TELFO...

NEWPORT

BROSELEY · LILLESHALL · SHIFNAL

CONTENTS

Red Books showing the way

Every effort has been made to verify the accuracy of information in this book but the publishers cannot accept responsibility for expense or loss caused by an error or omission.

Information that will be of assistance to the user of the maps will be welcomed.

The representation on these maps of a road, track or path is no evidence of the existence of a right of way.

Street plans prepared and published by ESTATE PUBLICATIONS, Bridewell House, TENTERDEN, KENT. The Publishers acknowledge the co-operation of the local authorities of towns represented in this atlas.

Ordnance Survey® This product includes mapping data licensed from Ordnance Survey® with the permission of the Controller of Her Majesty's Stationery Office.

www.ESTATE-PUBLICATIONS.co.uk

Printed by Ajanta Offset, New Delhi, India.

LEGEND

- Motorway
- 'A' Road
- 'B' Road
- Minor Road
- Pedestrianized / Restricted Access
- Track
- Built Up Area
- Footpath
- Stream
- River
- Lock — Canal
- Railway / Station
- ● Post Office
- Car Park / Park & Ride
- © Public Convenience
- + Place of Worship
- → One-way Street
- *i* Tourist Information Centre
- ▲8 ▲8 Adjoining Pages
- Area Depicting Enlarged Centre
- Emergency Services
- Industrial Buildings
- Leisure Buildings
- Education Buildings
- Hotels etc.
- Retail Buildings
- General Buildings
- Woodland
- Orchard
- Recreation Ground
- Cemetery

G000037658

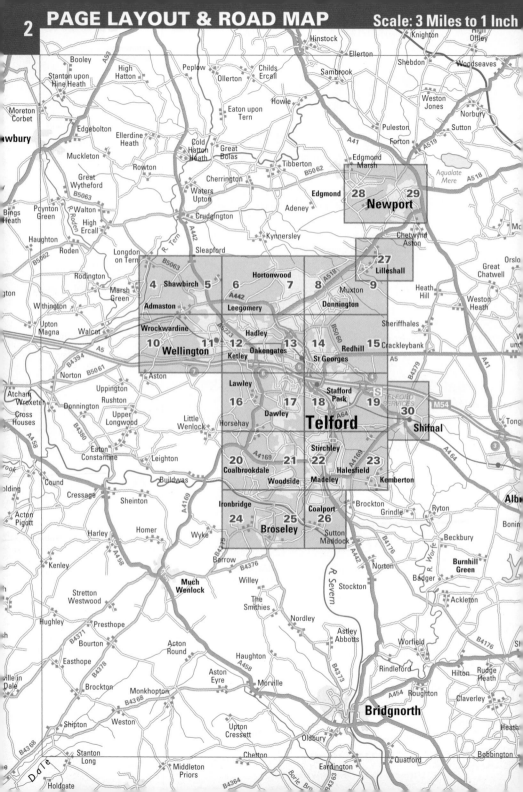

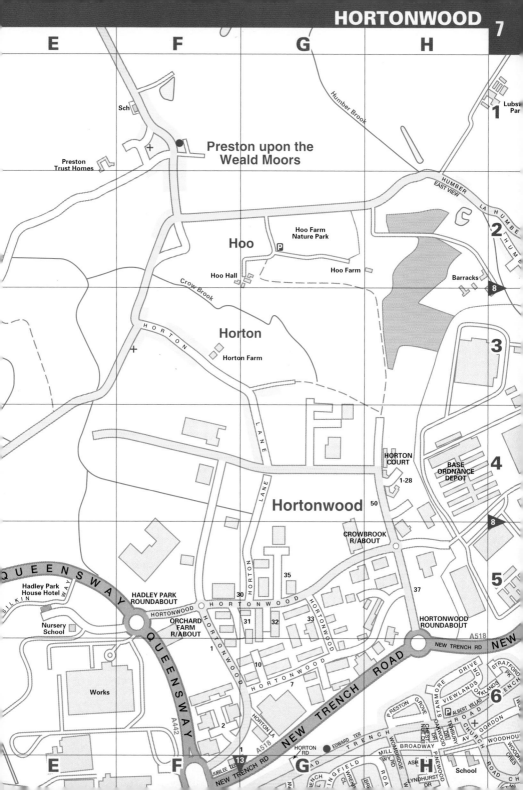

E F G H

1

Lubs
Par

Sch

**Preston upon the
Weald Moors**

Preston
Trust Homes

Humber Brook

HUMBER
EAST VIEW

HUMBER LA

HUMBE

2

Hoo

Hoo Farm
Nature Park

P

Hoo Hall

Crow Brook

Hoo Farm

Barracks

8

HORTON

Horton

Horton Farm

3

LANE

HORTON
COURT

1-28

**BASE
ORDNANCE
DEPOT**

4

LANE

Hortonwood

50

8

CROWBROOK
R/ABOUT

QUEENSWAY

Hadley Park
House Hotel

SILKIN WAY

Nursery
School

**HADLEY PARK
ROUNDABOUT**

HORTONWOOD

ORCHARD
FARM
R/ABOUT

HORTON

HORTONWOOD

30

35

31

32

33

37

**HORTONWOOD
ROUNDABOUT**

A518

NEW TRENCH RD

NEW

5

6

Works

QUEENSWAY

A442

HORTONWOOD

HORTONWOOD

1

10

7

2

HORTON LA

1

A518

NEW TRENCH ROAD

NEW TRENCH RD

JUBILEE TER

13

HORTON
RD

Edward Ter

TRENCH

GAD

INGFIELD CL

WREN

PRESTON
GROVE

JN

S

MORE DRIVE

VIEWLANDS

ALBERT VILLAS

OAKWOOD
ROAD

ROAD

BROADWAY

TENBURY

CHURCH

AV

WOMBRIDGE

MILL
WY

ASH

PINEWOOD

LYNDHURST
DR

STRATFORD

YKLANDS

GORDON

DEL

CREST

CL

WOODHOU

WOODHOU
CRE

ROAD

School

E F G H

Lilleshall

Honnington

Muxton

Golf Course

Kynnersley Drive
A518
NEW TRENCH RD
WELLINGTON RD

Monument
School
Cricket Grnd
Youth Centre
LIMEKILN LANE
WILLMOOR LANE
EAST
HILLSIDE
ST. MICHAELS CL
ROCK ACRES
CHURCH MDW
Cemy
Lilleshall Hall Farm
OLD FARM LA
ROAD

The Incline

Honnington Grange
YEW TREE DR
School
Old Hall
CHURCH ROAD
ABBEY
ELLINGTON
ROAD

Lilleshall Grange
The Oaks
ABBEY ROAD

Remains of Augustinian Abbey

Grange Cottages

Sulphur Piece Plantation

MUXTON LANESIDE
THE PADDOCK
GRANVILLE DR
STERLEY GRO
PERIVALE
CHALICE CL
CLIVE
MILLERS WY
NOBLES CVON
HOLLAND DR
MARSHBROOK
Sch
CANTERBURY
WINCHESTER CL
LYTHAM GRN
GRANVILLE DRIVE
RYDER DR
WAY WAY
WEYBOURNE
WR
CALDER
CHESTER
WR CALDER
LEIGH
GRO
MARSHBROOK

ROAD LILYHURST RD
Abbey Farm

Lilleshall Grove

The Shropshire P.H.
Golf Driving Range
RYDER LANE
Club House

Muxton Grange Cottages

Millingtons Coppice

New Lodge

E F G H
1
2
3
4
5
6
27
15

Ir Pla
Hu bri
27

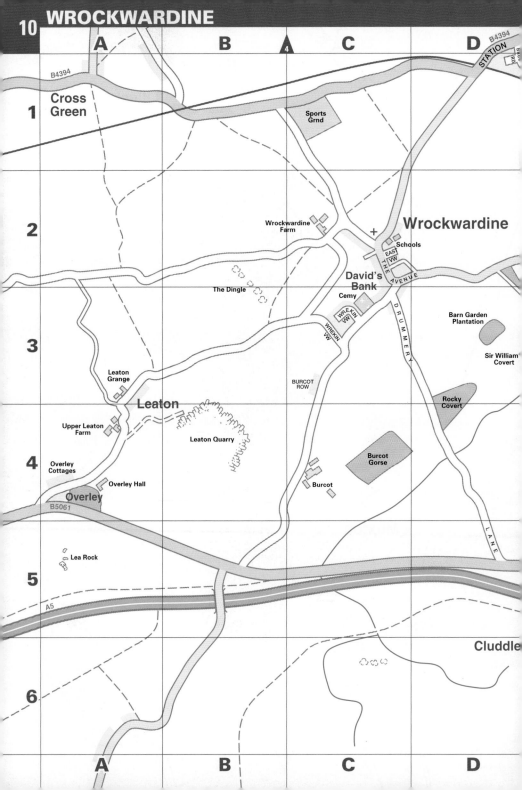

E F 9 G H New L

1

GRANVILLE ROAD

P ROAD

GRANVILLE

RANVILLE

GRANGE

Ferndale
Farm

*Granville
Country Park*

2

Cooper's
Coppice

ROAD

WOODHOUSE

Dawes
Bower

Woodhouse
Farm

LANE

3

LANE

GRANGE

Watling Street
Grange

Crematorium

LANE

4

VXACONA
Roman Settlement
(Site of)

Reservoir

ROMAN ROAD A5

NMEKILN BANK
ROUNDABOUT

WATLING STREET

Redhill

Redhill

INSBURY DR
MAYFAIR
WYNDHAM
GIRO
HOLBOURN
HIGHGATE CRES
LAMBETH RD
WEST
WESTMINSTER WAY

Upper
Woodhouse Farm

Woodgreen

5

ATCOMBE
COLLIFORD
Sch
HIGHGROVE MDWS
Medical
Centre
CHANCERY PK

Rec Grnd

ELTHAM DRI

YORK

WATERLOW
CL

HEREFORD AVE

SOUTH

WELL CL

AVENUE

ELY CL

CASTLE

AVENUE

ABELIA ARALIA
FUCHSIA
CAMELLIA
DR

CALLUNA
DR

FINCHLEY

SALISBURY AVE

LICHFIELD
CL

6

SWALLOWFIELD
CHILCOMBE
DR
LILYVALE
CL
KEW
GDNS

FARM

DRIVE

ADMAN
KESWORTH
DR

WOODHOUSE LANE

The Woodhouse

WAY

B5060

Wards Roughs

OPER

CASTL

19

E F WOOD G H

Playing

A • B • C • D

1

Steeraway

Short Wood

Arlesto Bill

Dawley Road

Lawley Furnaces

Kedley Brook

A5223

WLEY DR LAWLEY

2

Limekiln Wood

Silver Birches

School

DRI

GLENDALE AVE

SNG MWS

GLENDALE

TOM MORG CL

MILLMAN GRO

BARTHOLOMEW RD

3

Black Hayes

Birch Coppice

Lawley

HIGHFIELD

GLENDALE

GLENDALE

Playing Field

THE MEADOWS

WORKS LANE

NEW WORKS LANE

DAWLEY ROAD

New Works

CHURCH

HILL

Dawley Wellington Road

LAWLEY COMMON R/ABOUT

Footbridge

4

Lower Huntington Farm

Club House

LAWLEY

LAWLEY GAT

Horseha Commo

Golf Course

POC SIDE

NEW ROW

SPRING VILL

5

Huntington

DOG IN THE LANE

Horsehay Village Golf Course

Spring Village

SPRING VILL

POOL

Horseha Pool

POOL VIEW

Lyde Brook

WELLINGTON ROAD

Simpsons Pool

FARM LANE

6

Lydebrook Farm

Club

SIMPSONS CL

FARM MDW CL

R O A

IND EST

COALMOO

OR LANE

WOODHO

FORESTERS CL

BRIDGE

FRAM

ROAD

A5223

LANE

A • B • C • D

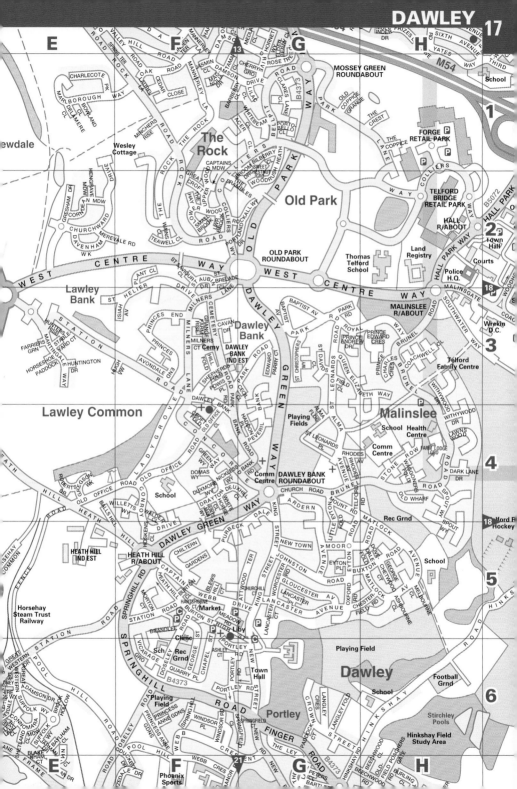

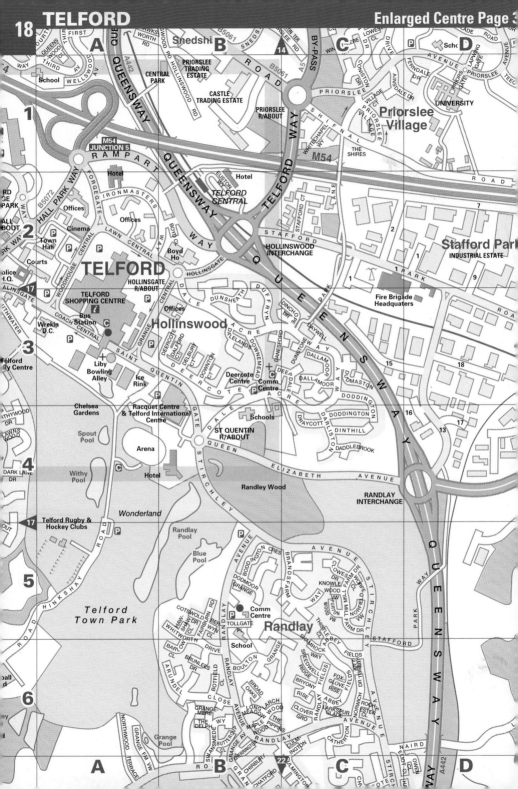

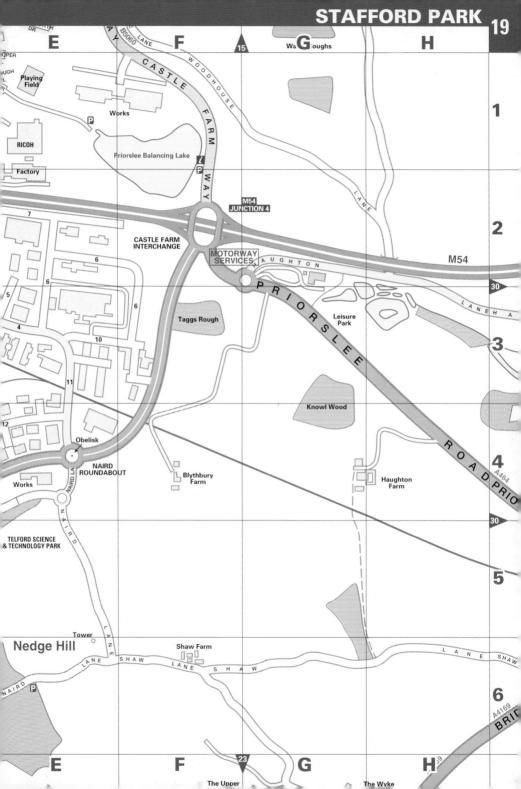

E   F   G   H

Woodhouse Lane

Wa Gloughs

15

1

Playing Field

Works

RICOH

Factory

Priorslee Balancing Lake

CASTLE FARM WAY

B5060

Lane

M54 JUNCTION 4

2

CASTLE FARM INTERCHANGE

MOTORWAY SERVICES

HAUGHTON

M54

30

7

6

6

6

5

4

10

Taggs Rough

PRIORSLEE

Leisure Park

LANE H A

3

11

Knowl Wood

ROAD PRIO

A464

4

12

Obelisk

NAIRD ROUNDABOUT

NAIRD LA

Blythbury Farm

Haughton Farm

30

Works

NAIRD

5

TELFORD SCIENCE & TECHNOLOGY PARK

LANE

Tower

Nedge Hill

Shaw Farm

LANE SHAW

LANE SHAW

6

NAIRD

SHAW LANE

SHAW

A4169

BRI

E   F   G   H

23

The Upper

The Wyke

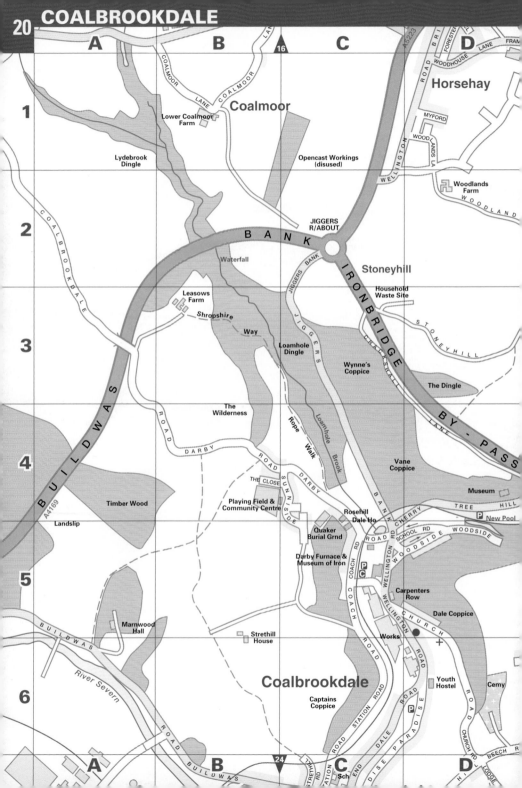

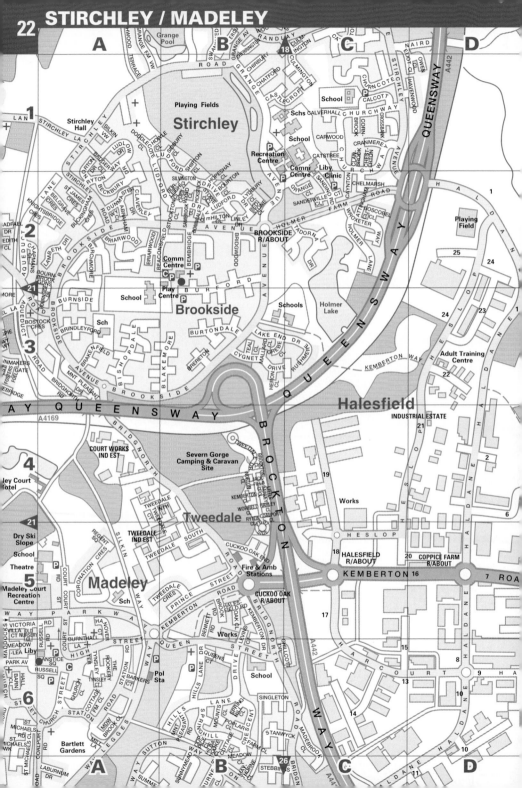

E F A G H

19

1

The Upper
Wyke Farm

The Wyke
Equestrian Centre

The Middle
Wyke Farm

The Wyke

A4169

Dodmoors

2

Old Mill Pond

Hem
Mill

The Hem
Farm

The Hem

LANE

Hem Manor
Farm

3

LANE

4

PADDOCK LA

FIELD

High Farm

GROOMS

KEMBERTON ROAD

5

West Ridge

HALL

Church
Farm

LANE

LANE

GRINDLE RD

Kemberton Hall
Farm

Kemberton

MILL

Clews
Wood

B4379

GRINDLE

ROAD

LANE

6

E F G H

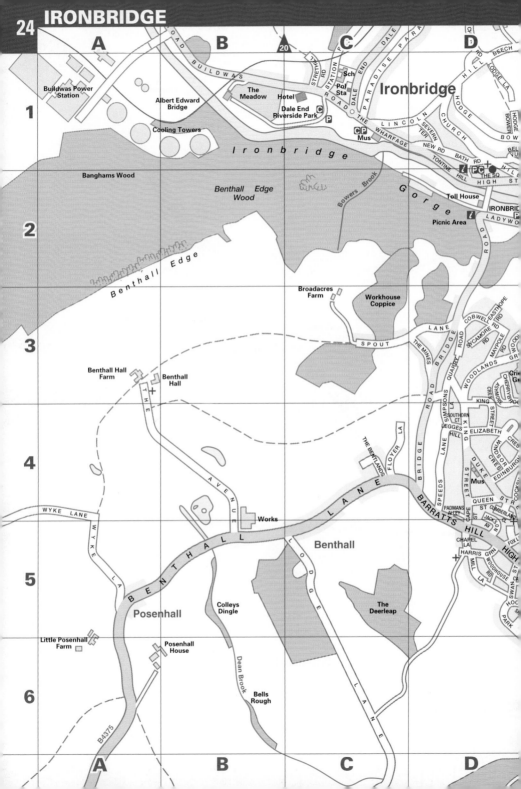

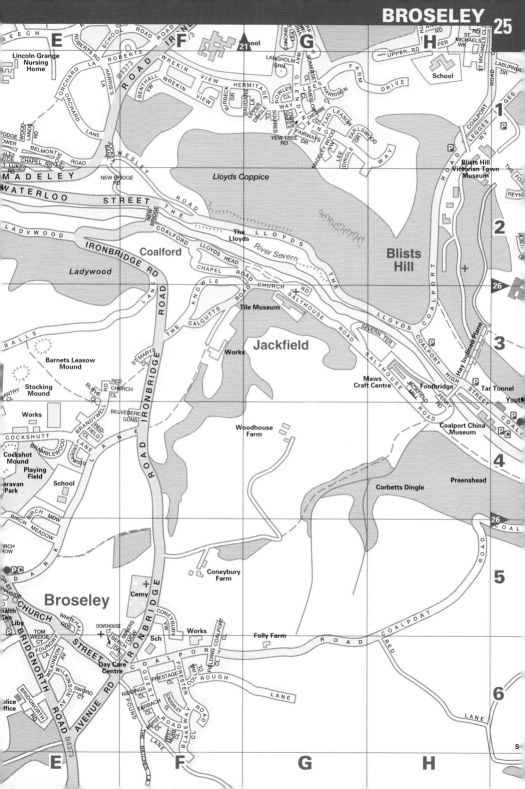

E F G H

Lincoln Grange Nursing Home

School

BEECH

ROBERTS RD

ROBERTS LA

SCHOOL RD

ROAD

IRONBRIDGE ROAD

School

LANGHOLM GRN

UPPER RD

St MICHAELS CL

St MICHAELS RD

LABURNUM DR

COALPORT LEGGES WY

HEDGES

P

1

ORCHARD LANDS RD

ORCHARD LANE

HARRIS'S LA

BENTHALL VW

WREKIN VIEW

WREKIN VIEW

HERMITAGE

BIRBECK DR

SAGGARS

SQUIRES LA

UPPER DINGLE

ROWLEY CL

GLENDINNING

CANNON RD

SOMERSET WAY

CLEMELLON CL

CHESHIRE

HARRISON CL

FARM DRIVE

B4373

WESLEY ROAD

JOCKEY BANK RD

YEW TREE RD

FAIRWAYS DR

MADELEY WOOD

FLAG LEASON

LEE DINGLE

EARLSWOOD WAY

Blists Hill Victorian Town Museum

P

LODGE LANDS RD

BELMONTE RD

CHAPEL RD

St LUKE'S

MADELEY

NEW BRIDGE RD

Lloyds Coppice

THE FOX

REYN

WATERLOO STREET

LADYWOOD

NEW BRIDGE RD

COALFORD ROAD

THE LLOYDS

River Severn

Blists Hill

COALPORT

ROAD

P

2

26

Ladywood

IRONBRIDGE RD

Coalford

LLOYDS HEAD

CHAPEL ROAD

The Lloyds

THE LLOYDS

THE

LLOYDS ROAD

COALPORT HIGH STREET

Hay Inclined Plane

26

BALLS

Barnets Leasow Mound

Stocking Mound

THE KNOWLE

THE CALCUTTS

St MARYS CL

CHURCH ROAD

Tile Museum

Works

SALTHOUSE ROAD

CHURCH RD

Jackfield

SEVERN TER

SALTHOUSE ROAD

Maws Craft Centre

Footbridge

JACKFIELD ROAD

JACKFIELD MILL

FERRY

STREET

Tar Tunnel

Youth

COAL

3

CANTRY CL

Works

COCKSHUTT

Cockshot Mound

BRAMBLEWOOD

Playing Field

School

RED CHURCH CL

BLITHE RD

BRANDYWELL LANE

BELVEDERE GDNS

RED CL

FIELD

Woodhouse Farm

IRONBRIDGE ROAD

Coalport China Museum

P

P

4

Caravan Park

BIRCH MDW

BIRCH MEADOW

Preenshead

Corbetts Dingle

ROAD

COAL

26

BIRCH ROW

PARK

Coneybury Farm

5

PC

Broseley

Cemy

CHURCH STREET

BRIDGNORTH STREET

WHITEHALL GDS

DOVEHOUSE CT

TOM WEDGE CT

BEECH

MINERS ROW

CONEYBURY RD

Sch

Works

Day Care Centre

WILKINSON AV

WILKINSON RD

SWORD CT

RIDDINGS CL

HURST CL

POUND LANE

THE LANE

BIRCHES RD

COALPORT ROAD

GUEST ROAD

PRESTAGE CL

AIRBACH CL

FORESTER CL

CAUGHLEY CL

FIELDING CL

BLAKEWAY

COLLIER ROW ROUGH

Folly Farm

ROAD

COALPORT

RED

LANE

LANE

S

AVENUE RD

BRIDGNORTH ROAD

B4373

Police Office

P

 health can

Liby

E F G H

6

A map of the Coalport area showing street names and landmarks. Notable labels include:

Bartlett Gardens, Sutton Hill, Clinic, Liby, Comm Centre, School, Sandcroft, Brockton R/About, Sutton Hill R/About, Playing Field, Brockton Court, Sutton Wood, Blists Hill Victorian Town Museum, Telford Hotel Golf & Crountry Club, Great Hay Golf Course, Sutton Hill Farm, Sutton Hill House, Brickkiln Coppice, Monarchs Way, Tar Tunnel, Youth Hostel, Coalport, Riverside Av, Coalport China Museum, Greensshead, High Street, Sutton Wood Farm, Coalport Bridge, Coalport Road, Sweyney Cliff, Sweyney Cliff House, The Wilds, River Severn, Sutton Wood, Caravan Site, Rowton House, Sewage Works, Tarbatch Dingle, Swinbatch, Bridgnorth Road, A442, Haldane, Hay Inclined Plane

Grid references: A, B, C, D across the top and bottom; 1, 2, 25, 3, 4, 25, 5, 6 down the sides.

Coates Pool

Little Hales Manor Farm

Little Hales Bridge

LILLESHALL HALL NATIONAL SPORTS CENTRE

Abbey Wood

Incline Plantation

Hughs bridge

The Incline

Remains of

New House Farm

Lilleshall

SYLVAS TO

BARRACK LANE

LIMEKILN LANE

WILLMOOR LANE

LANE

LANE EAST

Youth Centre

OLD FARM LA

LIMEKILN

School

Cricket Grnd

Lilleshall Hall Farm

Monument

HILLSIDE EAST

HILLSIDE

ST MICHAELS CL

CHURCH MDW

ROCK ACRES

ROCK ACRES

Cemy

Lilleshall Grange

ABBEY

ROAD

ABBEY

School

Old Hall

YEW TREE DR

ABBEY ROAD

CHURCH ROAD

Brockton Leasows

CHESWELL DRIVE

WELLINGTON ROAD A518

WELLINGTON RD

gton ge

gton

ROAD WELLINGTON A518

A he Oaks

A **B** **C** **D**

1

B5062
New Inn Farm
Newport Showground

SHREWSBURY ROAD

CHETWYND ROAD

LONGWITHY LANE

2

SHREWSBURY ROAD

WOODRIDGE CL

MENTONE CRES

CHETWYND ROAD

NEWPORT RD

NEWPORT

FLATT RD

HILLSIDE

STACKYARD LANE

Flatt Pit Farm

PIPERS LANE

MANOR RD

Sch

STREET

BAYLEY HILLS

ROBIN LANE

NEWPORT LANE

Windy Meadows Farm

Tickethouse Lock

ROAD

3

KILVERT CL

ST PETERS WY

ROCK LA

TURNERS LA

CONNERS LA

SCHOOL RD

Sports Grnd

Edgmond

Rec Grnd

Sewage Works

HIGH

Edgmond Hall Residential Centre

4

Vauxhall House Farm

ROAD

MOORFIE

5

Bridge Farm

Church (rems of)

Longford

LONGFORD

Brook Cottage

Longford Mill Farm

Longford Hall

Pool Covert

6

Mill Wood

Watkins Covert

Aston Hill

Aston Hill Covert

A **B** **C** **D**

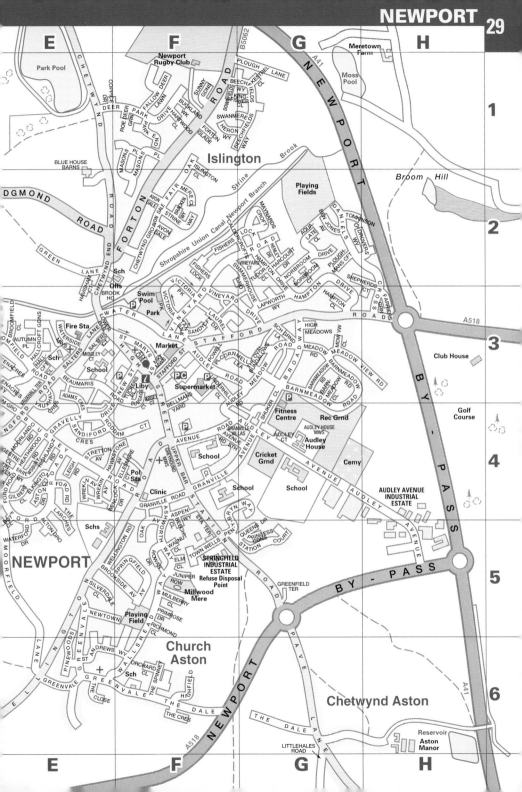

A B C D

1

Golf Course

M54

154

2

HAUGHTON LA

Wesley Brook

Haughton

19

Haughton Hall Hotel & Leisure Complex

3

Rec Grnd

BROOKSIDE DRIVE
WHEATFIELD
NEW-FIELD CL
OAKFIELD RD
BEECH DRIVE
SYCAMORE DRIVE
LABURNUM CL
WILLOW-DALE CT
MAPLE CL
BROADWAY
MERCIAN CT

HAUGHTON ROAD
WORFE RD
WOOLPACK CL
NEWPORT CRES
ORCHARD DRIVE

BROOKDALE DR
HIGH ST
PICK-WK
CURRIERS ST

MEADOW DR
ADMIRALS NO
WEST
COPPICE RD
DRAYTON RD
LOVELL
RODNEY CL
BARRINGTON CL
IDSALL DR
BARN
BOTFIELD ROAD

MNT-BATTEN
ADMIRALS WY
NELSON CT
BEATTY CL
BALFOUR RD
CORNWALLIS DR
JELLICOE CRES
WALLIS

COLLINGWOOD CT
ADMIRALS WY

Football Grnd

Idsall School

Shifnal County Primary School

ASTON CT MWS

Aston Hall

O A D PRIORSLEE A464 ROAD

Shifnal

Cemy

Cricket Grnd

THE LINDENS

HAUGHTON DR
THE PADDOCK
SHREWSBURY FIELDS
SPENCER COURT
SHREWSBURY RD

CHEAPSIDE
TUDOR
VICTORIA CT

BROADWAY HIGH ST
Liby
Pol Sta
Village Hall

GREENFIELDS CRES
GREENFIELD
GROSVENOR
GDS
BLUEGATE
ASTON ST
GREEN FIELDS
PINE-FIELDS
ASTON ROAD
LAWTON ROAD

STANTON LAMLEDGE ROA

4

19

SHAW LANE

A4169 BRIDGNORTH ROAD

INNAGE RD
VICTORIA RD
MARKET PLACE
PARK ST

WYKE
TALBOT CL
INNAGE CROFT
CARESWELL GDNS
WESLEY SCH
CHURCH
VICARAGE
MOAT
CROFT
MANOR
STAFFORD
TANGLEWOOD CL
APPLEBROOK
BRIMSTREE
COTTAGE DR
LODGE CL

ST JOHNS RD
THE GROVE
DYAS CL
BROOK LANDS AV
PARK LANE
PARK DRIVE

SHIFNAL
Sports Cen
MEAD WY
YEW TREE CT
STAFFORD CT
MERE CL
PARK
Hotel
SILVERMERE

THE OLD SMITHFIELD IND EST
SPRINGHILL TRADING ESTATE

SHIFNAL INDUSTRIAL ESTATE

New Park Farm

Revells Rough

5

A N F LANE

Wesley Brook

6

Mill Cottage

Lodgehill Farm

St Andrews Sch

Windmill (disused)

A464

A B C D

The Index includes some names for which there is insufficient space on the maps. These names are indicated by an * and are followed by the nearest adjoining thoroughfare.

32

Gate St TF2 14 B4
Gatehouse Cl TF1 6 A5
George Chetwood Ct TF4 17 H5
George P lTF1 11 G3
George St, Dawley TF4 17 F6
George St, St Georges TF2 14 B5
Gibbons Cl TF2 14 A1
Gibbons Rd TF2 8 A6
Gilbert Cl TF10 29 E4
Giles Cl TF5 5 F5
Gilpin Rd TF5 11 E1
Gilwell Gro TF2 14 D5
Gittens Dr TF4 21 G3
Glade Way TF5 5 F4
Gladstone St TF1 13 E2
Glebe St TF1 12 A4
Glebelands TF2 8 C6
Glen Cotts TF1 13 F4
Glenbrook Rd TF2 14 D6
Glendale TF4 16 D3
Glendale Gdns TF4 16 D2
Glendale Mews TF4 16 D2
Glendinning Way TF7 21 G6
Gleneagles Cl TF2 26 A2
Gloucester Av TF4 17 G5
Gloucester Ct TF1 6 C5
Glovers Way TF5 5 E4
Goldcrest Gro TF1 6 B5
Goldney Ct TF4 17 E6
Golf Links La TF1 11 H5
Gooch Cl TF2 21 E5
Goodrich Cl TF2 8 D4
Goodyear Way TF4 8 D6
Gordon Rd TF2 7 H6
Goshawk Dr TF1 6 A5
Gosling Pk TF5 5 G5
Gough Cl TF2 19 E1
Goulbourne Rd TF2 14 C5
Gower Cl TF2 8 D3
Gower St TF3 14 B3
Grainger Dr TF1 12 A1
Grampian Cl TF2 8 D4
Grange Av TF3 22 B1
Grange Central TF3 3 C5
Grange Cl TF3 22 C2
Grange Farm Rise TF4 17 F3
Grange Farm Vw TF3 18 A6
Grange La TF2 15 E1
Grange Rd TF2 13 H6
Grangemere TF3 18 B6
Granville Av TF4 29 F4
Granville Cl TF10 29 F4
Granville Dr TF2 9 E4
Granville Rd, Newport TF10 29 F4
Granville Rd, Telford TF2 14 C2
Granville St TF2 14 C4
Granville Villas TF10 29 F4
Grape Cl TF1 11 H2
Grasmere Cl TF2 14 C6
Gravel Leasowes TF4 21 E3
Gravelly Dr TF10 29 E4
Great Cft TF3 17 F2
Great Hay Dr TF7 26 A2
Great Western Dr TF4 17 E6
Grebe Cl TF3 22 B3
Green La TF10 29 E2
Green Way TF4 17 F4
Greenacres TF2 13 G5
Greenacres Way TF10 29 E3
Greenaway Pl TF2 8 A6
Greenfield Ter TF10 29 G5
Greenfields TF11 30 C4
Greenfields Cres TF11 30 C3
Greenfinch Cl TF1 12 A1
Greengage Way TF2 8 D5
Greenham Cl TF1 12 A4
Greenlea Rd TF2 13 H2
Greenvale TF10 29 E6
Greenwood Dr TF5 5 E5
Gregson Walk TF4 17 E4
Grenville Cl TF10 30 C3
Gresham Dr TF3 17 E2
Gresley Cl TF2 21 E5
Greyhound Hill TF2 13 H6
Greyhound Mws TF10 29 F4
Grindle Rd TF11 23 G6
Grinshill Flats TF1 11 G1
Grizedale Dr TF4 21 F1
Grooms Alley TF1 11 H3

Grooms La TF11 23 G5
Grosvenor Gdns TF11 30 C4
Grove Rd TF3 13 F6
Grove St TF2 14 B5
Grovefields TF1 12 D1
Guest Rd TF12 25 F6
Guests Cl TF2 8 D6
Guinea Cl TF2 14 A5
Guisbourne Av TF5 5 G4
Haddon Pl TF4 17 G4
Hadley Gdns TF1 6 C6
Hadley Lodge Rd TF1 13 F2
Hadley Park Rd TF1 6 C5
Hadley Pk Ind Est TF1 12 D1
Hadley Rd, Ketley TF1 13 F3
Hadley Rd, Oakengates TF2 13 G3
Hafren Rd TF4 21 F2
Halcyon Ct TF2 9 E4
Haldane TF2 22 D2
Halesfield TF7 22 C4
Halesfield Rd TF7 22 B5
Halifax Dr TF1 12 C1
Hall Barn Cl TF7 21 H6
Hall La TF11 23 E5
Hall Park Way TF3 3 A4
Hallcroft Cl TF10 29 E3
Hallcroft Gdns TF10 29 E3
Halldene TF1 12 C3
Hamilton Rd TF4 21 G1
Hamlet Cl TF2 13 H4
Hampton Cl TF10 29 G3
Hampton Dr TF10 29 G3
Hampton Hill TF1 11 G5
Hancocks Dr TF2 14 A5
Hanover Ct TF7 22 A5
Harcourt Cl TF7 22 C6
Harcourt Dr TF2 29 G2
Harding Cl TF2 8 A5
Harebell Glade TF3 18 C6
Harley Cl, Shawbirch TF1 5 G6
Harley Cl, Tweedale TF7 22 B4
Harp La TF4 21 G1
Harrington Hth TF5 5 F4
Harris Grn TF12 24 D5
Harrison Cl TF7 25 G1
Harrison Gdns TF1 12 B5
Harris's La TF8 25 E1
Hartley Cl TF3 13 F6
Hartsbridge Rd TF2 13 G5
Hartshill TF2 13 G4
Hartshorne Ct TF4 17 F5
Hartwood Cl TF10 29 F1
Harvey Cres TF1 12 C4
Harvington Cl TF1 11 H2
Haughmond Ct TF1 11 H1
Haughton Dr TF11 30 B4
Haughton La TF11 19 G2
Haughton Rd TF11 30 A2
Havenwood TF3 22 C1
Havisham Ct TF10 29 E3
Hawkshaw Cl TF2 14 A5
Hawkstone Av TF10 29 E4
Hawksworth Rd TF2 14 A6
Hawshaw Cl TF3 18 B5
Hawthorn Pl TF2 8 C5
Hawthorn Rd TF2 8 B5
Hawthorne Cl TF1 13 H6
Haybridge Av TF1 12 D3
Haybridge Hall Gdns TF1 12 C3
Haybridge Rd TF1 12 B4
Haybrook TF7 22 D6
Haycocks Cl TF1 5 G6
Hayes Rd TF1 12 B5
Haygate Dr TF1 11 F4
Haygate Rd TF1 11 F5
Hayward Av, Donnington TF2 8 C6
Hayward Av, St Georges TF2 14 B5
Hayward Par TF2 14 B5
Hazel Way TF2 14 B6
Hazelwood Dr TF4 21 G3
Heath Ct TF2 13 H4
Heath Hill TF4 17 E4
Heath Hill Ind Est TF4 17 E5

Heath Rd TF1 11 G2
Heather Dr TF1 12 B3
Heatherdale TF1 12 B1
Heathlands Cl TF2 14 B4
Heathwood Rd TF10 29 E4
Hedingham Rd TF1 6 D6
Hem La TF7 23 E3
Hendrie Cl TF1 13 E4
Hengrave Mdw TF3 17 E1
Henley Dr, Newport TF10 29 G2
Henley Dr, Telford TF2 14 A1
Herbert Av TF1 11 G4
Hereford Cl TF2 15 E5
Hermitage Way TF1 25 F1
Heron Cl TF3 22 B3
Heron Way TF10 29 F1
Hertford Cl TF1 12 A2
Hesba Cl TF1 11 G4
Heslop TF7 22 C5
Heywood Lonsdale Ct TF1 12 A4
Hiatt Av TF1 12 A2
High Mdws TF10 29 G3
High Mt TF2 14 B1
High St, Broseley TF12 24 D5
High St, Dawley TF4 17 F5
High St, Edgmond TF10 28 A3
High St, Hadley TF1 12 D2
High St, Ironbridge TF8 24 D2
High St, Madeley TF7 22 A6
High St, Newport TF10 29 F3
High St, Shifnal TF11 30 C3
High St, Wellington TF1 12 A3
Highfield, Newport TF10 29 F2
Highfield, Telford TF1 16 D3
Highgate Dr TF2 15 E5
Highgrove Mdws TF1 15 E5
Highland Lea TF4 17 E6
Highland Rd TF10 29 E4
Highway Vw TF1 12 C4
Hilda Hooke Cl TF7 22 B6
Hill Crest Rd TF4 14 B5
Hill Fold TF4 17 F3
Hill Rd, Dawley TF3 13 F6
Hill Rd, Donnington TF2 8 B2
Hill St TF2 14 B4
Hill Top Rd TF2 13 G4
Hills Lane Dr TF7 22 B6
Hillside, Edgmond TF10 28 A2
Hillside, Ironbridge TF8 25 E1
Hillside, Lilleshall TF10 9 F1
Hillside Cl TF1 12 B5
Hillside East TF10 9 G1
Hillside Rd TF2 13 H5
Hilton Cl TF3 22 B2
Hilton Ter TF2 14 A4
Hinkshay Rd TF4 21 G1
Hockley Rd TF2 14 D5
Hodge Bower TF8 24 D1
Holbourn Cres TF2 15 E5
Holland Dr TF2 9 E5
Hollies Rd TF1 11 G3
Hollinsgate TF3 3 C4
Hollinswood Rd TF2 3 C1
Holly Cl TF4 21 F2
Holly Rd TF2 21 F2
Hollybirch Gro TF2 14 B5
Hollyhurst Rd TF2 13 H2
Hollyoak Gro TF2 14 C5
Holme Cl TF1 12 A2
Holmer Farm Rd TF3 22 B2
Holmer La TF3 22 C2
Holt Coppice TF5 5 E5
Holyhead Rd, Ketley TF1 12 D4
Holyhead Rd, Oakengates TF2 13 G5
Holyhead Rd, Telford TF2 14 C2
Holyhead Rd, Wellington TF1 11 E5
Holywell La TF4 21 E3
Hookacre Ct TF2 14 C5
Hopeshay Cl TF2 22 B2
Hopkins Hth TF5 5 F4
Hordley Rd TF1 11 F1
Hornbeam Cl TF1 12 C4
Horne Rd TF2 8 B2
Hornet Way TF3 13 G6

Horsechestnut Dr TF5 5 G5
Horsehay Common TF4 17 E5
Horseshoe Pad TF4 17 E5
Horton Cl TF1 7 H4
Horton La TF1 7 G5
Horton Rd TF2 7 G6
Hortonwood TF1 7 F5
Hoskens Cl TF4 17 F5
Houlston Cl TF2 14 C3
Houseman Cl TF3 21 H2
Howle Cl TF3 22 A1
Hudson Cl TF2 14 A2
Hugh Vw TF2 17 E3
Humber La TF2 7 H2
Humber Way TF2 8 A2
Hunters Rise TF4 17 E3
Huntington Dr TF4 17 E3
Huntsman Way TF4 17 F4
Hurleybrook Way TF1 12 C2
Hurst Cl TF12 25 F6
Hutchinson Way TF1 13 E5
Hyde Cl TF2 8 D4
Ice House Cl TF1 6 A6
Idsall Cres TF11 30 C3
Ingestre Cl TF10 29 E4
Innage Cft TF11 30 B5
Innage Rd TF11 30 B5
Innes Av TF2 13 H5
Iris Cres TF2 14 B3
Ironbridge By-Pass TF4 20 C2
Ironbridge Rd, Broseley TF12 25 F6
Ironbridge Rd, Jackfield TF8 25 E2
Ironbridge Rd, Telford TF7 21 F6
Ironmasters Way TF3 3 B2
Ironstone Cl TF2 14 C5
Isiah Av TF4 17 F3
Islington Cl TF10 29 F1
Ivatt Cl TF4 21 H1
Ivor Thomas Rd TF2 14 C6
Ivy Gro TF1 11 G4
Ivy House Pad TF1 13 E3
Jabe Davies Cl TF2 14 B6
Jackfield Cl TF7 22 B4
Jackfield Mill TF8 25 H3
Jackson Av TF12 24 D4
James Cl TF2 14 A1
James Clay Ct TF1 12 D3
James Nelson Cres TF2 8 A6
James Way TF2 8 A6
Japoncia Dr TF1 6 C6
Jarman Dr TF4 17 E6
Jasmin Cl TF3 17 F1
Jay Dr TF1 12 A1
Jellicoe Cres TF11 30 C2
Jethros Cft TF10 29 G1
Jiggers Bank TF4 20 C3
Jockey Bank TF8 25 E1
John Broad Av TF1 12 A5
John St TF11 30 B5
John Stone Cl TF2 14 B2
Johnston Rd TF4 17 G5
Johnstone Cl TF2 14 A4
Joseph Rich Av TF7 21 H6
Jubilee Av TF2 8 C4
Jubilee Ter TF1 13 F1
Juniper Dr TF2 8 B2
Juniper Row TF10 29 F5
Kearton Ter TF1 13 F3
Keepers Cres TF2 14 C3
Kemberton Cl TF7 22 B4
Kemberton Dr TF7 22 B5
Kemberton Rd TF7 22 B5
Kemberton Way TF7 22 C3
Kensington Way TF2 13 H4
Kenwray Dr TF2 14 C6
Kestrel Cl TF10 29 G1
Kestrel Cl TF1 12 B1
Kesworth Dr TF2 15 E6
Ketley Bsns Pk TF1 13 E5
Ketley Town TF1 13 E5
Ketley Vallens TF1 13 E4
Kew Gdns TF2 15 E6
Kilvert Cl TF10 28 A3
King St, Broseley TF12 24 D4
King St, Dawley TF4 17 G4
King St, Wellington TF1 11 H2
Kingfisher Cl TF10 29 F1

Kingfisher Way TF1 12 A1
Kings Ct TF1 12 A3
Kings Haye Rd TF1 11 H4
Kingsland TF1 12 B1
Kingsley Dr TF2 8 C4
Kingston Rd TF2 13 H1
Kingsway Cres TF1 12 B5
Knightsbridge Cres TF3 21 H2
Knowle Wood Vw TF3 18 C5
Kynnersley Dr TF10 9 E1
Laburnum Cl TF11 30 B3
Laburnum Dr TF7 26 A1
Laburnum Rd TF3 13 H3
Ladbrook Dr TF2 14 B5
Ladycroft TF1 11 H2
Ladygrove TF4 17 F4
Ladywood TF8 24 D2
Lake End Dr TF3 22 B3
Lambeth Dr, Redhill TF2 15 E5
Lambeth Dr, Stirchley TF3 22 A2
Lamledge La TF11 30 D4
Lancaster Av TF4 17 G5
Lancaster Ct TF4 17 G5
Lancaster Pl TF4 17 G5
Landy Cl TF2 8 B3
Laneside TF2 9 E4
Langer Cl TF2 14 C4
Langholm Grn TF7 25 G1
Langley Cres TF4 17 G6
Langley Fold TF4 17 F6
Lapwing Gate TF2 18 D1
Lapworth Way TF10 29 G3
Larch Wood TF3 18 B6
Lark Rise TF2 14 B3
Larkspur Glade TF3 18 C6
Laurel Dr TF2 29 F3
Laurel La TF3 17 F1
Lawford Cl TF4 21 G3
Lawley Dr TF1 12 D6
Lawley Gate TF4 16 D4
Lawn Central TF3 3 B3
Lawndale TF2 8 B5
Lawns Wood TF3 3 A6
Lawrence Rd TF1 11 F3
Lawton Farm Cl TF1 6 B6
Lawton Farm Way TF1 6 B6
Lawton Rd TF11 30 C4
Lea Cl TF4 12 A2
Leadon Cl TF4 21 F3
Leasowe Grn TF4 21 F3
Leaton Dr TF1 11 G2
Lee Dingle TF7 25 G1
Leegate Av TF1 6 C6
Leegomery Rd TF1 11 H2
Lees Farm Dr TF7 25 G1
Leeses Cl TF5 5 F4
Legges Hill TF12 24 D4
Legges Way TF7 22 A6
Leicester Way TF1 12 B2
Leigh Rd TF10 29 E4
Lennock Rd TF2 8 A6
Leonard St TF2 13 H4
Leonards Cl TF2 8 B6
Leveson Cl TF2 14 A4
Levins Ct TF7 22 B6
Ley Brook TF2 13 F4
Lhen Cl TF2 8 D5
Lichfield Cl TF2 15 F6
Lidgates Green TF1 12 C5
Lightmoor Rd TF4 21 F4
Lilac Cl TF3 17 G1
Lilyhurst Rd TF10 9 H4
Lilyvale Cl TF2 15 E6
Lime Tree Way TF1 12 A2
Limekiln Bank TF2 14 C4
Limekiln La, Newport TF10 27 B1
Limekiln La, Wellington TF1 12 A4
Limes Walk TF2 14 A4
Lincoln Cres TF2 14 A3
Lincoln Hill TF8 24 C1
Lincoln Rd TF2 14 A3
Linden Av TF1 11 G4
Linden Gro TF1 11 G4
Linden Ter TF3 13 F6
Lindfield Dr TF1 12 C5
Lineton Cl TF2 14 A1
Linley Dr TF3 22 B2
Linnet Gate TF1 5 F5

Place	Ref
Telford Bridge	
Retail Pk TF3	**3 A3**
Telford Rd,	
Malinslee TF4	17 G4
Telford Rd,	
Wellington TF1	11 G5
Telford Science &	
Technology Pk TF11	**19 E5**
Telford Shopping	
Centre TF3	**3 B4**
Telford Way TF3	3 D3
Teme Av TF1	11 F1
Ten Tree Cft TF1	11 H3
Tenbury Dr TF2	7 H6
Teresa Way TF1	12 B1
Tern Cl TF4	21 F3
Tern Way TF1	11 G1
The Avenue,	
Broseley TF12	24 A3
The Avenue, Telford TF6	10 C2
The Beeches TF5	5 E6
The Bentlands TF12	24 C4
The Border*, Telford	
Shopping Centre TF3	3 B4
The Brambles TF3	17 F2
The Bungalows TF3	8 C4
The Cloisters TF2	13 H3
The Close,	
Newport TF10	29 E6
The Close, Telford TF8	20 B4
The Common TF2	8 C6
The Coppice TF3	17 H1
The Court TF7	26 A2
The Crescent,	
Newport TF10	29 F6
The Crescent,	
Telford TF2	8 C5
The Crest TF3	17 H1
The Crofts TF5	21 E5
The Dale TF10	29 F6
The Delph TF3	18 B6
The Fields TF2	8 D5
The Finger TF4	21 G1
The Foxes TF4	26 A1
The Grove,	
Shifnal TF11	30 C5
The Grove, Telford TF1	12 D1
The Grove Est TF2	14 B5
The Hay TF3	17 F2
The Hollow*,	
King TF4	17 G5
The Incline TF1	13 E5
The Knowle TF8	25 F3
The Larches TF10	29 E4
The Lawns TF1	11 H2
The Ley TF4	17 G6
The Lindens TF11	30 B4
The Lloyds TF8	25 F2
The Maltings TF1	11 G3
The Meadow TF2	13 H5
The Meadows TF4	16 D3
The Mines TF12	24 D3
The Nabb TF2	14 B3
The Old Smithfield	
Ind Est TF11	**30 C4**
The Oval Bungalows	
TF10	29 G3
The Paddock,	
Shifnal TF11	30 B4
The Paddock, Telford TF2	9 E4
The Parade,	
Donnington TF2	8 B5
The Parade,	
Wellington TF1	11 H3
The Pippins TF3	18 B6
The Rock TF3	17 F1
The Rookery TF7	22 A6
The Saplings TF7	21 E5
The Savannahs TF1	5 H6
The Shires TF1	18 C1
The Spinney,	
Newport TF10	29 F6
The Spinney,	
Telford TF2	8 D4
The Square TF8	24 D2
The Stables TF2	9 E4
The Stocking TF4	21 E3
The Sutherlands TF2	8 D3
The Timbers TF2	8 D3
The Wharfage TF8	24 C1
The Woodlands,	
Oakengates TF2	14 A3
The Woodlands,	
Wellington TF1	13 F6
Thetford Chase*,	
Telford Shopping Centre	
TF3	3 B4
Third Av TF2	3 B1
Thirlmere Gro TF2	14 C6
Thistle Cl TF3	18 C5
Thornton Park Av TF2	9 E4
Toll Rd TF1	12 C5
Tollgate Pl TF3	18 B5
Tom Morgan Cl TF4	16 D3
Tom Wedge Ct TF2	8 C5
Tomkinson Cl TF10	29 G2
Tontine Hill TF8	24 D1
Town Wells TF10	29 F5
Townsend Cft TF2	8 C4
Trafalgar Cl TF2	8 C3
Trench Cl TF2	13 G1
Trench Lock TF1	13 F1
Trench TF2	13 F1
Trenleigh Gdns TF2	13 H1
Trevithick Cl TF7	21 F5
Trinity Rd TF4	21 F1
Trinity Vw TF2	13 H5
Troon Way TF7	26 A2
Tuckers Pl TF10	29 F3
Tudor Cl TF10	29 G2
Tudor Mdw TF2	13 G1
Tudor Way TF11	30 C4
Turbervill Cl TF2	14 C3
Turners La TF10	28 A3
Turnpike Cl TF4	14 B4
Turnstone Dr TF1	12 C2
Turreff Av TF2	8 B5
Tweedale Cres TF7	22 A5
Tweedale Ct TF7	22 A4
Tweedale Dr TF7	22 B4
Tweedale	
Ind Est TF7	**22 A5**
Tweedale North TF7	22 A4
Tweedale South TF7	22 A5
Tynsley Ct TF7	22 A4
Tynsley Ter TF7	22 A6
Ullswater Cl TF2	14 C6
Underhill Cl TF10	29 F3
Undertrees Cl TF1	5 G6
Underwood TF12	25 E4
Union Ct TF1	13 E2
Union Rd,	
Oakengates TF2	14 A3
Union Rd,	
Wellington TF1	11 H4
Union St TF1	13 E2
Uplands Av TF2	13 H4
Upper Bar TF10	29 F4
Upper Dingle TF2	25 G1
Upper Rd TF7	25 H1
Upper Wood TF3	17 F2
Urban Gdns TF1	12 B4
Urban Rd TF2	14 A3
Urban Ter TF2	14 B4
Urban Villas TF2	14 B4
Urban Way TF1	12 B4
Valley Rd, Arleston TF1	12 B5
Valley Rd, Overdale TF3	13 E6
Vauxhall Cres TF10	29 E4
Vauxhall Ter TF10	29 E4
Verbena Way TF7	26 A2
Vicar St TF2	13 H5
Vicarage Dr TF11	30 B5
Vicarage Gro TF4	21 F3
Victoria Av, Ketley TF1	12 D4
Victoria Av,	
Wellington TF1	12 A3
Victoria Ct, Shifnal TF11	30 B4
Victoria Ct, Telford TF1	12 A3
Victoria Mews TF1	12 A3
Victoria Pk TF10	29 F2
Victoria Rd,	
Madeley TF7	21 H5
Victoria Rd,	
Shifnal TF11	30 B4
Victoria Rd,	
Wellington TF1	11 H3
Victoria St TF1	11 H3
Viewlands Dr TF2	7 H6
Villa Ct TF7	21 H5
Village Cl TF2	13 H4
Village Ct TF2	18 C1
Village Way TF2	13 G4
Vineyard Ct TF10	29 G2
Vineyard Dr,	
Newport TF10	29 F3
Vineyard Dr, Telford TF1	11 H3
Vineyard Pl TF1	11 G2
Vineyard Rd,	
Newport TF10	29 F3
Vineyard Rd,	
Telford TF1	11 H3
Violet Cl TF2	8 D5
Viscount Av TF4	21 H3
Wade Rd TF2	14 A1
Wadham Cl TF1	12 A2
Waggoners Fold TF3	17 H4
Wagtail Dr TF4	21 H3
Wains Cl TF3	17 F2
Walder Cl TF4	17 F4
Walker Cres TF2	14 B4
Walker St TF1	11 H3
Wallshead Way TF10	29 F6
Walney Ct TF7	21 F5
Walnut Cl,	
Newport TF10	29 F5
Walnut Cl, Telford TF4	21 H3
Walsh Cl TF2	14 D5
Walton Ct TF2	13 G1
Waltondale TF7	21 G5
Wantage TF7	21 G4
Warrensway TF7	21 E6
Warwick Way TF1	6 D6
Water La TF10	29 E3
Waterford Dr TF10	29 E5
Waterloo Cl TF1	13 E3
Waterloo Rd, Ketley TF1	13 E2
Waterloo Rd,	
Wellington TF1	12 A3
Waterloo St TF8	25 E2
Waterlow TF7	15 F5
Waterside Mws TF10	29 E3
Watling St TF1	12 B4
Waverley TF7	21 H5
Wavertree Cl TF2	14 B5
Waxhill Cl TF2	14 C1
Wayside TF7	21 G5
Wealdstone TF7	21 F5
Weavers Rise TF2	17 F6
Webb Cres TF4	17 F6
Wedgewood Cres TF1	12 D3
Weir Gdns TF1	13 E2
Wellington Ct TF1	11 H4
Wellington Rd,	
Admaston TF5	5 E6
Wellington Rd,	
Coalbrookdale TF8	20 C5
Wellington Rd,	
Donnington TF2	8 A5
Wellington Rd,	
Horsehay TF4	16 C5
Wellington Rd,	
Lilleshall TF2	9 E3
Wellington Rd,	
Newport TF10	29 E6
Wellsfield TF7	21 G5
Wellswood Av TF2	3 B1
Wenlock Ct TF7	21 F5
Wenlock Dr TF10	29 E4
Wentworth Dr TF4	21 G3
Wesley Av TF11	30 B5
Wesley Dr TF2	13 H5
Wesley Rd TF8	25 E1
West Av TF2	8 A6
West Centre Way TF4	17 E2
West Rd,	
Oakengates TF2	13 G5
West Rd,	
Wellington TF1	11 G4
West St TF2	14 B5
West View Ter TF7	21 G6
Westbourne TF7	21 F6
Westcroft Walk TF2	14 C5
Westerdale Cl TF4	21 F1
Westerkirk Dr TF7	21 G6
Western Rise TF1	12 D4
Westminster Way TF2	15 E5
Westmorland Mws TF1	12 C2
Weston Cl TF11	30 C2
Weston Dr TF1	11 G2
Weybourne Walk TF2	9 E5
Weybridge TF7	21 E5
Weyman Rd TF1	11 G2
Wharf Cl TF2	14 B4
Wheatfield Dr TF11	30 B3
Wheatley Cres TF1	12 D1
Wheeldale Cl TF4	21 E1
Whimbrel Cl TF1	12 C2
Whinchat Cl TF1	12 A1
Whitchurch Dr TF1	5 G5
Whitchurch Rd TF1	5 H6
White Horse Cl TF4	17 F4
Whitebeam Cl TF3	17 G1
Whitechapel Way TF2	18 C1
Whitehall Gdns TF12	25 E5
Whitemere Dr TF1	11 G2
Whiteway Dr TF5	5 E5
Whitmore Cl TF12	25 F6
Whitworth Dr TF3	18 B5
Wicket Cl TF2	14 D4
Widewaters Cl TF4	21 G3
Wigeon Gro TF1	6 B6
Wigmores TF7	21 G5
Wild Thyme Dr TF2	8 D5
Wildwood TF7	21 F5
Wilkinson Av TF12	25 E6
Willetts Way TF4	17 E4
Williams Rd TF2	8 B2
Willmoor La TF10	27 C2
Willow Bank TF1	21 H3
Willow Rd TF2	14 A4
Willowdale TF11	30 B3
Willowfield TF7	21 G4
Wilmere Ct TF7	21 F5
Wilton Ct TF7	21 F5
Winchester Dr TF2	9 E5
Windermere Dr TF2	14 C6
Windsor Cres TF12	24 D4
Windsor Flats*,	
Windsor Rd TF1	12 C4
Windsor Pl TF7	17 F6
Windsor Rd,	
Arleston TF1	12 C4
Windsor Rd,	
Dawley TF4	17 F6
Winifreds Dr TF2	8 B6
Winston Dr TF2	8 C5
Withington Cl TF2	13 H3
Withybrook TF7	21 E5
Withywood Dr,	
Malinslee TF3	17 H3
Withywood Dr,	
Telford TF3	3 A5
Wolverley Ct TF7	21 F5
Wombridge Hill TF2	13 G3
Wombridge Rd TF2	7 H6
Wombridge Way TF2	13 G4
Wood Cl TF2	14 B1
Woodbine Dr TF2	8 D5
Woodcroft TF7	21 G5
Woodford Grn TF5	5 E4
Woodhall Cl TF5	5 E5
Woodhouse TF2	8 A6
Woodhouse Central TF3	3 A4
Woodhouse Cres TF2	8 A6
Woodhouse La,	
Granville TF2	15 G2
Woodhouse La,	
Horsehay TF4	20 D1
Woodhouse La,	
Priorslee TF2	15 E6
Woodhouse La,	
Redhill TF2	14 D5
Woodhouse Rd TF12	24 A3
Woodland Villas TF2	14 A3
Woodlands Av TF1	11 F3
Woodlands Cl TF12	24 D3
Woodlands Grn TF12	24 D3
Woodlands La TF4	20 D1
Woodlands Rd TF8	25 E1
Woodpecker Cl TF1	6 C5
Woodridge Cl TF10	28 B1
Woodrows TF7	21 G5
Woodrush Hth TF3	17 G2
Woodside TF8	20 C5
Woodside Av TF7	21 E5
Woodside Cl TF1	13 E5
Woodside Rd TF1	13 E5
Woodspring Gro TF2	9 E5
Woodwell TF1	13 G5
Woollam Rd TF1	12 C4
Woolpack Cl TF11	30 B3
Worcester Rd TF4	17 G5
Wordsworth Way TF2	14 C6
Worfe Cl TF3	18 C5
Worfe Rd TF11	30 B2
Worfield Cl TF7	22 B4
Wrekin Av TF10	29 E4
Wrekin Cl TF2	13 G1
Wrekin Ct TF1	11 H5
Wrekin Dr TF2	8 B5
Wrekin Rd TF1	11 H4
Wrekin	
Retail Pk TF1	**12 C5**
Wrekin Vw,	
Madeley TF7	25 F1
Wrekin Vw,	
Wrockwardine TF6	10 C3
Wrekin Walk*,	
Telford Shopping Centre	
TF3	3 B4
Wrens Nest La TF1	13 E5
Wrockwardine Rd TF6	11 E2
Wrockwardine Wood Way	
TF2	13 H2
Wroxeter Way TF3	22 C2
Wych Elm Dr TF5	5 G5
Wyke La TF12	24 A4
Wyke Rise TF1	12 A2
Wyke Way TF11	30 A4
Wyndham Gro TF2	15 E5
Wyvern TF7	21 E6
Yates Way TF2	13 H6
Yellowstone Cl TF2	14 B3
Yew Tree Cl TF11	30 C5
Yew Tree Dr TF10	9 F2
Yew Tree Rd TF7	25 G1
York Rd TF2	15 F5

THEY
THOUGHT
THEY WERE SAVED

G000037590

5
**Born-again Christians
recall a startling discovery.**

PENFOLD BOOKS

Contents

3

Preface

In one of the most solemn portions of the Bible, the Lord Jesus Christ refers to *a large number of people* who, to their own great surprise, are shut out of the kingdom[1]. By so saying, He had no intention of undermining the faith of true believers. It was simply a much-needed warning about those who merely 'professed' to be saved but in reality had never known Him. In the whole universe of time and space, could anything be more tragic than dying — expecting to awake in heaven — only to end up in outer darkness? Small wonder that Christ speaks of weeping, wailing and gnashing of teeth.

If you do some asking around, you will discover many who claim to be born again but who speak in the following terms:

"I don't ever remember being saved."
"I cannot recall my salvation but my parents say they remember it."
"I never had a Damascus Road conversion; I suppose you could say I have always believed."
"Because I was raised in a Christian home it is difficult for me to point to a conversion experience."
"I've always believed Christ died for me, but I can't recall a point in time when I was saved."

This type of talk is encouraged by a conscious trend within modern evangelicalism, which is replacing a long history of preaching that emphasises 'crisis conversion', with a new style that encourages 'gradualism' in personal salvation. Yet, as all would acknowledge, no one can be half or a quarter saved. Each human being is either completely saved or totally lost. So there must be a point in time to which salvation can be traced.

With eternity at stake, laxity about conversion is a deadly thing. Yet churches often let candidates for baptism and church fellowship pass without a proper enquiry regarding personal salvation, or a hollow story of salvation is accepted rather than cause an upset. But the New Testament teaches that each convert to Christ must have had a conversion. While no fuss is made about remembering a *date* on the calendar, the conversions in the Bible were all memorable experiences. The actual date is immaterial; but the experience of personally exercising faith in Christ is essential.

True, a child's conversion is not usually as dramatic as an adult's conversion. However, a child's conversion is a profound event. How could a child turn from Satan to God, from darkness to light and from death to life and be oblivious of the transaction? How could the entrance of the Holy Spirit into the life be less memorable than a multitude of lesser childhood memories, such as holidays and Christmas presents? Forgetting your conversion experience due to Alzheimer's disease is totally understandable. But what we are talking about here is a sizeable group of evangelicals who *have never been able to recall being saved.*

False profession — thinking or saying one is saved when one is not — acts like a vaccination because, while it lasts, it inoculates the soul against true conversion. The false professor is self-deceived. Christian friends may unwittingly compound the problem by taking the professing Christian's conversion for granted. The telltale signs are not detected, because the assumption overrides them.

A word of warning is called for at this point. We are not seeking to over emphasise 'the experience' above the reality. The Bible does not call upon us to trust an experience — only to trust in Christ. We are only too aware of another enormous group of people who can point to an experience in their life which they identify with

6

being born again – but there is not the slightest evidence of the work of God in them and no fruit has ever been seen in their life. They walked an aisle, said a 'sinner's prayer', signed a decision card or had hands laid on them and spoke in 'tongues', but they have never truly repented and trusted in Christ. They were never once awakened to see their condemnation and never learned the meaning of soul trouble[2]. They are trusting a 'decision' — but have not trusted in the Lord Jesus. Such people are not saved – no matter how many experiences they have had. It is by their fruits that we know people have been born again. That said, trusting in Christ is an experience and an unforgettable one at that.

If, after reading this book, you find that you identify with the testimonies, please do not think that your case is impossible to unravel. If you discover that you are not saved, the important thing is to admit it to God immediately and seek true salvation without delay. God will never turn away the truly repentant sinner who is seeking salvation. No embarrassment here on earth is so great that it can be compared with sleep walking into hell. If it was only for time it would not be serious, but *this is for eternity*. Examine yourselves, whether you are in the faith or not[3].

1. Luke 13v24-30   2. Acts 2v37   3. II Corinthians 13v5.

7

IF IT'S GOOD ENOUGH FOR HIM

by
Stuart Jamieson

The problem was, I could never remember when, where or how I had become a Christian. I had never had an experience, which could be recalled and described as 'being saved'. As a child I had stood up for Christianity, but since a child is so impressionable and I was merely expressing views instilled during my upbringing, in reality it meant little to me.

When I was twelve years old, a well-respected Christian teacher came for a series of meetings to the Gospel Hall where our family attended. One night, at our home, when asked to tell his conversion experience, he replied *"I do not have one, all I know is that I am trusting Christ."* That completely surprised me, but I thought to myself, *"If that is good enough for him, it is good enough for me."* From then on I relied on this, another man's story, as the basis for believing that I was a true Christian.

The belief that I was a genuine Christian was reinforced during a summer Christian Camp I attended. I was put in with the team called 'the Lords', as opposed to 'the Commons', on the grounds of the assessment by others that I was a Christian — despite the fact that I had never vocalised a clear experience of being born again. I was baptised at 13 years of age and received 'into fellowship' at the Gospel Hall. Eventually I started preaching the gospel myself.

However all the time I had doubts and fears about my salvation and wondered if Jesus Christ came back for his people, as he had promised, would I really go with them to heaven? Had I real evidence of the work of the Holy Spirit in my life? Despite these overwhelming concerns I never had the courage to confide in anybody.

University shock

In 1975 I left home to study at University. It was full of highly intelligent people and I was bewildered by the strange assortment of 'Christians' there. I joined with the believers at another Gospel Hall a few miles from the University and was quite amazed by their enthusiasm for witnessing to others about their faith. At University, studying the Bible, in fact even reading it, increasingly became a chore. It was simply another form of academic pursuit. Prayer was a struggle, becoming more and more difficult until it eventually degenerated into a regular recitation, much like a shopping list.

At the beginning of February 1976, I travelled in the back of a car with a full time Christian worker from Holland who was on a visit to the Gospel Hall. He told me his story of becoming a Christian and simply asked for mine. I told him that I did not remember ever becoming a Christian but I believed I was one. I shall never forget his reply: *"Do you not remember a time of assurance even? [What] a strange story."* I was most indignant as to the right of this man to just about question my salvation, but God had spoken to me in no uncertain terms.

From then on, at the various services, I scrutinised lines of hymns when they were sung. Since I did not want to sing lies, words of well known songs such as 'Oh happy day' or 'What a wonderful change' were impossible for me to sing. I could not truthfully relate to a happy day, nor speak in retrospect of there ever having been a wonderful change in my life.

On the 14th February that same year, I was stunned when a 30-year-old man, who was part of the same fellowship as me and a very regular attendee at the services for many years, 'got saved'. He was another one who, like me, had never been able to remember the day of his supposed conversion. He had enjoyed the company of the Christians and attended many meetings, yet he had come to realise that he had been unsaved the whole time. This was the first case of an unsaved person 'in fellowship' that I had ever come across. However, God spoke to me through five more similar cases in the following six months. A few weeks later, after a particular meeting, this newly converted man asked me for my testimony and by doing so just about finished me for that weekend!

I began to search the Bible for verses which explained what ought to be the evidences of a real Christian who possessed the Holy Spirit. I could not honestly claim to have such evidences in my life. In fact, the Bible was no help to me in these circumstances – rather, it troubled me. I became afraid to ask anybody about their conversion story in case they asked for mine in return.

Easter

During the Easter holiday, the agony began to get worse. While visiting Manchester I stayed with some Christian friends. I was scared that anybody would ask me how I had been saved. I was invited by one of my friends to join him on a visit to see a young man who was interested in being saved. I went reluctantly, not out of interest for his spiritual welfare. While there my friend told his personal story of how he had become a Christian. Unwittingly he was speaking to me as well. Personal testimonies were becoming a bit of a nuisance — I kept hearing them! At about the same time, I

11

heard of two people in the United States who had been in fellowship with Christians at a Gospel Hall for 20 years and had discovered that they were not saved.

I returned to University for the summer term intending to settle down to take my examinations, but I was still bothered. Any new convert was talked to guardedly! A special series of evangelical meetings was taking place but I had no enthusiasm for them. I was petrified that either of the two evangelists would enquire about my salvation. Even a message by one of them one evening on 'How I know I am saved' did not help. I was even given a lift to one of the meetings by a man who lived in the town where they were being held — but I just could not bring myself to invite him to them. I could not understand it then but I can now.

For my interest I was given a rather sombre and old-fashioned tract called 'The Final Witness'. It began, "*Nothing is more reliable than death-bed testimonies — then even liars are forced to tell the truth.*" I read the deathbed testimonies of those who had been saved and did not feel I could say their kind of words if I were dying. God spoke through that tract but I did not really want to listen.

The fact is, I was really in agony about the fact that I had simply never had a personal encounter with Jesus Christ. I was glad to get home, and away from those believers, after the end of year examinations. I had been home about a week when a speaker from a nearby city came to preach in my hometown. He spoke of the disciple Peter's experience of sinking in the sea and crying out, "*Lord save me*". He closed his message quite simply with words to the effect: "*Do you think Peter could ever forget that day? Would it be possible for Peter to never remember the day when he had been saved ?*" I did not hear much more. This seemed to be directed straight at me although the preacher did not know it. By now it had reached the point, as things became worse and more uncomfortable, that I really did not want to be with other Christians. About the same time, a few friends and myself went to tea with one of the local preachers. While chatting in the garden he quite casually said, *"Don't be discouraged in gospel preaching when there are only 'church people' present, because I am sure there are many in churches who are not saved. Why, you had a case like that when you were at University quite recently"* [referring to the 30 year old man I mentioned earlier]. It was as if God would not leave me alone even when I went out to tea! While walking in town a few days later, I went into a bookshop to browse. I picked a book up and opened it. The frontispiece read: *"This man, like so many others, found Christ while at University"*. That was too much. I walked out.

Radio

I could not even turn the radio on. Twice (the exact dates I cannot remember) I innocently turned on the radio to listen to the news and on two separate occasions was disturbed by what I heard. Once when a group of Wimbledon tennis players had been talking to newsmen about their 'personal experience' with Jesus Christ, and another time when a man involved in the Watergate affair talked of a change in his life since meeting Jesus Christ. I was at last beginning to break.

The week before going back to the Gospel Hall near the University for a week of Bible teaching and outreach, I strengthened myself by intending to stick to my story of being a Christian. As soon as I arrived the issue started to haunt me again. In that week I heard at least eight quite different personal testimonies, each of which disturbed me because they shared one common factor — all spoke of a definite experience with God. I heard no testimony to which I could in any way relate and feel comfortable with. To heighten all this, the wife of the Dutch evangelist was there too. How I wanted to avoid her!

In the mornings we studied the letter to the Romans. There the apostle Paul explains the truth of the gospel. Paul made it clear that when Abraham believed God it was a point in time when God accounted righteousness to him. Faith saves, but there must be a deliberate act of putting faith in Christ for salvation. This was how the Bible teaching spoke to me and I could not get away from it. Even the Apostle Paul's conversion came up in the form of *"It is hard for you to kick against the goads"*, a quotation from his experience on the road to Damascus. It was explained to be the goading of his conscience by the Holy Spirit.

During the afternoons the young people went out evangelizing. I accompanied them in fear rather than with zeal. One afternoon a young lad recounted to me how, while knocking on doors, he had met a young woman who told him that because she was baptised she was saved. He had replied, *"And **when** were you saved?"* The door had been slammed in his face but I was being spoken to again. Then one of the visiting Christians told all of us young lads who were sat together at tea how *"the soul business is the business to be in"*, meaning it was worthwhile to engage in evangelizing. I knew I could never do that. I then realised that I had no desire to bring others to Christ, nor was I pleased for those who had recently been converted.

I did not want to talk to anybody and tried to be alone but got no peace. I began to really examine my life. Towards the end of the week one of the evangelists took *'Remember Lot's wife'* as the text for his message. He recounted how Lot's wife walked with the people of God but went to hell. He thus concluded that it was possible to walk with God's people but not be saved. He then recounted how amazed he was when a Sunday School teacher came to him one night after fifteen years in fellowship who had realised he was not saved. This was the fourth case of its kind which had come to my recent attention and it really sank home afterwards, when somebody also told me of a man who was convicted and converted while preaching his own gospel message! If it could happen to these people it could happen to me. The evangelist also showed how that similarly Cain talked to God but went to hell. He thus deduced it was also possible to talk with God and yet not be saved.

The next night I sat at the front, to the side of the speaker, and to make things worse the Dutch woman was just about opposite me. The preacher took three questions from the book of Jeremiah, one of which made me think deeply. It was *"What wilt thou say when he shall punish thee ?"* from Jeremiah chapter 13 v 21. I answered it in my own mind; *"Oh God, I thought I was trusting, but I have never come to repentance."* At about the same time I realised that it was not a matter of satisfying other people about my salvation — it was a matter of being satisfied myself that everything was settled between God and myself. No one else mattered. I was glad to get away from those meetings on the Sunday afternoon; I felt pursued!

Sleepless nights

Once I had returned home, I started reading articles about assurance of salvation, but they were no use. On Monday morning I walked into the town in a complete daze. I told myself I was at my wits' end; I had come to the end of myself. I was doing some work as a student and it was night shift that week. I was troubled for the whole 12 hours of the shift and then at home was not able to get much sleep for worry. I was so concerned about spiritual matters that from Monday morning until Friday evening I had only 20 hours sleep. On the Monday night I realised I had been academically studying the word of God just like any other subject. As soon as I realised this the Bible started preaching to me.

Three verses kept returning to me the whole week. They were:

John 3 v 5 - *"Except a man be born of water and of the Spirit he cannot enter the kingdom of God."*

Luke 13 v 5 - *"Except ye repent ye shall all likewise perish."*

Acts 17 v 30 - *"God commands all men everywhere to repent."*

With these scriptures turning over in my mind I thought of all the conversions in the Bible. Nicodemus, the woman at the well, Paul, the Philippian jailer; all felt their need and experienced change in their lives. I looked at my life carefully. I was still the same. No change had ever taken place. I realised then that I was a sinner by habit, always losing the battle with conscience. I had been taught the truth while young and just accepted it with never any repentance, never any recognition of need and never any change of life. To me this now seemed impossible since being 'born again' is supposedly the greatest thing that can happen to a person. I was not happy to meet God as I was.

Peace at last

These things plagued my mind continually. I prayed for help. Finally I arranged to meet one of the elders from the Gospel Hall near the University. I drove slowly all the way, just as I had worked so carefully all week, in case anything happened to me. I arrived mentally exhausted at 9 o'clock in the evening. The man was not there. 15 minutes later I got out of the car and wandered aimlessly around the car park talking to myself — *"I do not know why I am here, it is so obvious that I need to be saved."* Things flashed through my mind. I thought, *"The Holy Spirit and the Word of God have been speaking to me for six months. My life does not show any personal effect of the scriptures. I have no enthusiasm for evangelism. I am pretty indifferent to sin and have no real power over it."* Still my confidant did not arrive. Was it possible that at this latest tortured moment of my life the Lord Jesus Christ had returned for his people and I had been left behind?

I got back into the car not being able to stand it any more, bowed my head over the steering wheel and confessed everything to God. I repented of everything as a sinner and asked for the revolution in my life that I longed for. I asked God for the blood of Christ to cleanse me. Yet I did not feel any different. I asked for assurance. It came quite suddenly in the form of a verse I knew. It was I John chapter 1 v 7 which says *"The blood of Jesus Christ His Son cleanseth us from all sin"*. In that moment I placed my trust and absolute belief in that verse and the Saviour of which it spoke and immediately the burden of the months was gone.

I looked up and my friend had arrived. I went and told him. We talked over the wonder of the new birth and how we do not know the workings of the Holy Spirit nor *"how the bones grow in the womb"* (Ecclesiastes 11v5). Going home I was so happy — full of real joy. It was Friday the 13th August 1976 and I was at long last a different person.

Since then I have realised the awful solemnity of the words of Christ when He said, "Not every one that saith unto me, Lord, Lord, shall enter into the kingdom of heaven; but he that doeth the will of my Father which is in heaven" (Matthew 7v21). I leave this with you and trust it may speak to any reader who is like I was before my true conversion.

IT WAS ALL FOR ME

by
David Armstrong

I was born, one of a family of two boys, in the village of Waringstown in County Down, Northern Ireland. My father and mother sought to bring us up in the fear of God. Their prime object in life was the spiritual salvation of their little family and they did what they could to shield us from ungodly influences around us. I can never recall a time in life when I did not know that I was a sinner on the way to hell, and that it was God's desire that I should be saved and live forever in heaven. Although from an early age, due to my godly upbringing, I really was 'spoiled for the world', in reality I was no different from others in seeking my own way and neglecting the all-important matter of 'my soul's salvation'.

As young children we were encouraged to learn the Word of God off by heart. In early years we were able to recite many of those well-known gospel passages and verses of scripture. In addition, we were taught basic Bible principles, including our need as sinners, and God's wonderful provision in the death of his beloved Son. I will never forget those tears, as night after night Father or Mother would pray with us before we retired to sleep.

Of course there were times when we coveted the 'freedom' that others of our age seemed to enjoy — freedom to go to places of worldly amusement and participate in a whole range of worldly pursuits. While we never openly refused to go to gospel meetings, or Sunday School, we simply longed for the day when we would be old enough to get away from home and every semblance of parental restraint, to enjoy something of what the world had to offer. In fact it was against this background that I intimated to my parents, on one occasion, that I would like to join the Merchant Navy.

God speaks

God was gracious to me and from a very early age I heard His voice through various means. Others would be 'saved' who I knew very well. Then there was personal sickness and accidents; not forgetting deaths and funerals among family and friends. As I reached the age of understanding, I never recall attending a series of special gospel meetings without having some thought of where I would spend eternity. I always dreaded the thought of the return of Christ at any moment, and many were the occasions when I actually thought that this mighty event had possibly taken place. In addition, there was the ongoing fear that the Holy Spirit would cease to 'strive' with me and leave me in my sins to perish eventually, as He did with some I heard about in the Bible.

Looking back over those early years in Waringstown, I regret that I was not saved at 11 years of age. A 16-year-old cousin of mine was saved in Tent Meetings at the edge of the village conducted by Messrs. Thomas McKelvey and Thomas Wallace. The preachers stayed in our home during those meetings and the presence and power of God was realised in a way that I fear is seldom experienced today. When I saw the effect that salvation had on my cousin Irene, I determined to seek it as well. Unfortunately the meetings ended with me still in my sins. Then, at 19 years of age, Irene died and went home to be with Christ! What a mercy that she was saved in the tent three years earlier!

In 1950, Mr. William Bunting came to the village for gospel meetings. At 13 years of age I was more determined than ever to be saved. I attended the meetings and with each succeeding evening the realities of eternity increasingly troubled me. I thought I knew how to be saved — but not any more. I listened with rapt attention night after night and tried to pray, to trust, and to believe but to no effect.

Towards the end of the meetings, Mr. Bunting recounted his own story of salvation and how God had used the words of Romans chapter 10 and verse 9 in his own enlightenment. The verse reads *"That if thou shalt confess with thy mouth the Lord Jesus and shalt believe in thine heart that God hath raised him from the dead, thou shalt be saved."*

I could hardly wait to get home from the meeting and into my bedroom with my Bible. I tried to pray, asking God to save my soul as I had been doing for a number of weeks. Once in bed I opened my Bible at Romans chapter 10 and read verses 9 and 10. As I read over the words of verse 9, I thought to myself, *"If this is good enough for a man like Mr. Bunting, it is good enough for me!"* Immediately I got out of bed, knelt down and thanked God for saving me. Of course there was great rejoicing in the home that night.

Doubts

For a good while all seemed to go well, but with the passage of time, my interest in my Bible and the things of God began to wane. I had a number of problems in relation to my experience. When I heard someone claim that they were as sure of going to Heaven as if they were already there, I had to acknowledge within myself that I couldn't make that claim — but why not? To me, salvation had become a disappointment, if not a sham. I was in the unenviable position of trying to live the life of a Christian, while at the same time longing to enjoy the company and life of the unsaved. Of course the unsaved did not want my company since I professed to be a Christian! I could have used the words of the apostle Paul in another context, "*O wretched man that I am!*" Reluctantly I began to ponder the possibility that I had something I had often heard about and dreaded — 'a false profession'. But what was I going to do? Graciously, God proved to be in control and His wisdom, love and patience were once again displayed.

Mr. Bunting came to Bleary for some more Tent Meetings in the summer of 1953. As usual I was expected to attend these meetings and did so nightly. It wasn't long until my peace was shattered. I was beset with doubts as to the reality of my salvation. To make matters worse, the preacher seemed to emphasise the reality of true salvation and the awful possibility of someone having a counterfeit experience. He underlined the fact that, while it may be possible to deceive some of our fellow men, it would be impossible to deceive God — he said solemnly, "*only reality will stand the test*".

Matters came to a head one Sunday night during the meeting. During his remarks Mr. Bunting stated clearly that God would not keep anyone in the dark as to how they stood in relation to salvation. He went further and suggested that anyone in doubt should apply the following test: "*Ask yourself in the presence of God, 'Have I got a love for the Lord Jesus?'.*" With an honest heart I applied the test there and then and came to the conclusion that I could not answer in the affirmative. I concluded "*I'm not saved at all.*" The preacher called at our home that night and asked how I was. I told him that I had found out in the meeting that I wasn't saved. He didn't seem taken by surprise but advised me there and then to seek salvation right away.

The meetings finished and I was still not saved. At the end of the meetings I did something that I had never done before — I made a vow to God that if He would send some preachers within reach again, I would seek salvation with all my heart. If there is one thing more miserable than living the life of the unsaved, it is living the life of a false Christian!

Oh the love of God! Instead of leaving me as I was in my sins, He sent his servant, Mr. Bunting, for a further series of gospel meetings to the village of Donacloney, approximately three miles from where we lived. Immediately I was brought face to face with my vow to God. If I did not honour it, there was every possibility that I would never have another chance. Thus, before the meetings actually commenced I reconfirmed my vow to God and made up my mind to seek God's salvation at these meetings. God certainly spoke to me, but the more I tried to get salvation, the darker I seemed to become. Eventually, one night after the meeting, Mr. Bunting asked me if I was saved yet. When I answered *"No"*, he responded with words that touched me deeply: *"Well, David, I'm afraid you are going to miss it this time."* This was like an arrow from God. I was convinced beyond all doubt that this was one of the last, possibly *the* last, opportunity I would ever have of being saved.

Revelation

In the home that night I tried to pray, trust and believe, but once again without any relief. Now, the tears seemed to dry up and I made my way down to the kitchen. Mr. Bunting called in and prayed with me and left the home. I made my way back up to the sitting room and walked around the room, my mind blank. Suddenly I began to think of John chapter 5 v 24. I went over to the couch and on my knees opened my Bible and began reading the following words: *"Verily, verily, I say unto you, He that heareth my word, and believeth on him that sent me, hath everlasting life."*

As I read, the tears began to flow. I thought of the place called

Calvary and the sufferings of the Lord Jesus Christ on the cross. At that point I was no longer trying to trust or believe — simply pondering. Just at that moment the truth dawned upon me for the first time with clearness and in simplicity as follows: *"And why did the Lord Jesus suffer? Ah, sure, it was all for me!"*

I had made one mistake — I did not want to make another. I pointed with my finger at each word I had read. I was entirely satisfied. I had God's infallible word! For the very first time I truly thanked God for saving me. What a joy it was to wake up in the morning, turn again to the Bible and read the entire verse, including the phrase *"and shall not come into condemnation, but is passed from death unto life."*

I have often been asked what is the difference between this experience and that in 1950. It is all the difference in the world! In 1950 I looked to a verse of Scripture that God had used in the experience of someone else. I had tried to have *his* experience and to enjoy *his* assurance. On 5th November 1953, by faith, I came to Christ, the person in John 5v24, and had an experience all of my own.

God's salvation means more to me now that it ever did. I can say in the language of another, *"We love him, because He first loved us"*, *"Yea, He is altogether lovely."* What a joy to know that all is well for eternity and to anticipate the moment when I will meet my Saviour face to face. I sincerely hope this testimony will be a blessing to the reader.

A HANDSHAKE FOR ETERNITY

by
Linda Matthews

It is amazing how we can be deceived! Sometimes it is self-deception — other times it is the work of the 'great deceiver', Satan. In my case I suppose it was a combination of both. I certainly was a willing participant, but deep down in my heart, I never wanted to be deceived about the salvation of my eternal soul. In I John 5v13 it states, *"That ye may know that ye have eternal life, and that ye may believe on the name of the Son of God."* By the grace of God, I now know the joy of salvation through the Lord Jesus Christ. I am resting in the finished work that He accomplished for me on the cross — and this is how it all happened.

My earliest memories as a child growing up definitely include an awareness of God. Although I did not grow up in a home with Christian parents, each night before going to sleep, I would pray *"Now I lay me down to sleep, I pray the Lord my soul to keep, if I should die before I wake, I pray the Lord my soul to take."* This prayer was like a lucky charm to me. The ritual of saying it made me feel safe, although it did not always chase away the frequent bad dreams. One dream in particular has stayed with me through the years. I was about seven years old when it occurred. In the dream I was playing out in the field behind our home. I came upon a hole in the ground. Just as I bent down to peer into the hole, the Devil came out of the hole and began talking with me. He said he had been watching me and wanted me to go down into the hole with him. At that point I woke up the whole family, screaming in terror. I knew I didn't want to go with the Devil! Occasionally my parents would send us children to a church programme like Sunday School or what we called Vacation Bible School. They wanted us to learn about God and to know right from wrong, but that was the extent of our 'religion'.

Florida

When I was 13 years old, the family moved to Florida. We had just moved into our new home, when some Christians visited us from the nearby Baptist Church. My mother was impressed by their friendliness and decided to visit the church the next Sunday. When Sunday morning arrived, she got all six of us children up to go with her. This was new — we were used to going fishing with our Dad on Sundays! After that first visit Mum decided that we would be attending on a regular basis. One Sunday morning something exciting happened at Church. The preacher was talking about Jesus who had died on a cross for the sins of the world. At the end of his message, he told us that we needed to make a decision. He gave an invitation for anyone to walk to the front of the building and join the church. My mother walked down the aisle that morning. I decided to follow her. I didn't understand what I was doing but I trusted that someone would explain to me when I got down the aisle. The preacher shook my hand and simply said, *"We will baptise you next week."*

At the end of the service, the whole church came down to shake me by the hand and congratulate me on being 'being saved'. The next Sunday, we went to a local lake, where my Mother and I were baptised. Although I still had questions in my mind about what had actually happened, I didn't say anything to anyone. I presumed they must have known I was truly saved since they were willing to baptise me. For the next four years, this was 'my salvation'. On Sundays I went to Church and sang the great hymns of the faith. Then for the rest of the week, I lived my second life. Away from my Mother and the Church, I was another person altogether. In Genesis 6v5 it says, *"Every imagination of the thoughts of his heart was only evil continually."* This verse sums up the way I was on the inside. On Friday night I might be taking part in a seance to contact the spirits of the dead, but on Sunday morning I would be singing in the choir. I thought I had everyone fooled. In reality there was only one fool — me.

In my Junior year of High School, when I was 16 years old, a group of girls had planned to go to a film one particular Friday night. My Mother would not let me go, preferring that I attend a Youth Rally at our church instead. I went to the Youth Rally. That night, as my friends were driving out of the Cinema Car Park, a lorry hit them. Sandra, the driver of the car, was killed instantly. All the other girls were severely injured. Had my mother not insisted that I go to the Youth Rally, I would have been in that car. As the tragedy sank in I realised that if I had died that night, I would have gone to hell. I put the thought out of my mind, closing it to reality.

Boyfriend

Later that same year, just after my 17th birthday, I met a young man who was to have a huge impact on my life. A friend of mine, who had joined the U. S. Air Force, came home for a visit and brought this young man with him. Although I already had a boyfriend who everyone was assuming I would marry, when I met Buck Matthews, no one else mattered. We started dating each time he managed to obtain leave from the Air Force, usually between weekends. We wrote letters. The occasions when Buck visited on a weekend he would go to church with us on Sundays. He had been raised in the Roman Catholic Church, and to come to our church was, in his eyes, a sin against his religion — so he would sit and listen, but did not take part in the singing or other church activities. Interestingly, at that time, our church had a new preacher, Mr. Hamel, who Buck really related to, because he too had been raised as a Roman Catholic.

Buck had only been coming to our church for about 4 or 5 Sundays, when one Saturday night, while we were on a date, he asked me a question: *"What would you think if I walked forward at church, not this Sunday, but the next?"* I replied that if he was doing it for me I wouldn't think anything of it! He was surprised at my answer. The next morning, as we were standing side by side in church, Buck began to cry. Now it was my turn to be surprised. Right there beside me that morning, Buck Matthews came to know the Lord Jesus as his personal Saviour. From that moment on, he was a changed man — and the reality of the change in him began to work on me. He could not get enough of the Bible! He just wanted to serve the Lord and this desire affected his whole life. How different he was from me — yet I was the one who was supposed to teach him how to live for Christ! We had regular 'soul-winning' efforts in our church, when we went out knocking on doors and seeking to lead people to Christ. I taught Buck how to do 'soul-winning' and went with him as often as I could.

Several months went by, and we continued writing to each other between visits, I began to see that the changes in him were undeniable. Often in the stillness of my bedroom at night, I would find myself lying awake questioning the genuineness of my own 'salvation' experience. About this time, our Bible Class teacher gave our class a book to read about the Second Coming of Christ. The title of the book was *Raptured* and the author was Ernest W. Angley. As I started to read, I found I could not put the book down. It was as if I was reading my own life story.

28

In the book, a young girl who knew how to be saved, refuses salvation, and is left behind when Christ returns for His own people. She has to face the horror of living during the time of tribulation that comes on the earth. It was a Wednesday night and I was almost at the end of the book. By this time, there was no denying what I now knew in my heart was the truth. Quite simply I had never come to know the Lord Jesus as my Saviour. I was convicted in my conscience. As the book ends, the lost are calling for the rocks and the mountains to fall on them and hide them from the face of God. I saw myself there, in all my lost condition. As the burden of my sin overwhelmed me, I could hardly read the last words on the page. I fell to my knees and cried out to the Lord Jesus to save me. Just as the Lord Jesus reached out and pulled Peter from the sea as he cried out *"Lord save me!"* so my Saviour came to the rescue that night.

The peace that He brought *"through the blood of His cross"* (Colossians 1v20) became mine that night. Immediately I wanted to tell everyone. I drove to the home of the Pastor of our church to give him the news. To say he was surprised would be an understatement! As we talked further, he could see the change in me. There was now a new life evident in my heart. In I John 4v13 it says, *"Hereby we know that we dwell in Him and He in us, because He hath given us of His Spirit."* The emptiness that I had known for so long was gone. I am so glad the Lord did not leave me in my lost condition. In spite of my repeated attempts to shut Him out of my mind, still He called to me. The most amazing thing of all is that when I finally called out to Him, He was there to save me. *"Whosoever shall call upon the name of the Lord shall be saved"* (Romans 10v13). To this day, no matter what circumstances life has brought to me, my Saviour has been with me. He has promised, *"I will never leave thee, nor forsake thee"* (Hebrews 13v5).

"MOTHER, I'M NOT SAVED"

by
Ken Magennis

What a privilege was mine — to be born in a country where gospel preaching was very common and where I learned from my earliest days that I needed to be saved if I was ever to enter Heaven. How can I begin to estimate the worth of a mother who taught the word of God to her children from their youngest years, and who, each Sunday, walked with us to the Gospel Hall (three miles there and back) in Drumlough, Northern Ireland.

Travel arrangements were such that when I went to College, I had to move to the town of Banbridge. There I lived with my godly old grandmother. Along with my Aunt and Uncle, we all attended the Baptist Church in Banbridge, not only on Sundays, but also on Wednesday evenings. During my teenage years it was quite common for evangelists to come to Ulster from America and conduct gospel campaigns in a similar fashion to the famous Billy Graham Crusades. A group of young people from my Church regularly attended these meetings and found them exciting. It was common practice at such meetings that, when the sermon was over, an appeal was made to the audience to 'come forward and trust Christ'. One particular evening I felt moved to respond during the appeal — so I went forward. There I met the preacher who took his Bible and read some suitable Scriptures with me. He then asked me if I wanted to trust Christ as my Saviour. I said

"Yes". The preacher told me to pray and invite the Lord Jesus into my heart. I closed my eyes, bowed my head and said 'the sinner's prayer'. When I finished, the preacher spoke some words of assurance to me and, in order to help me confirm my commitment and to help preserve me from future doubts, asked me to sign a 'decision card' which I kept from that day forward.

Sceptical

My family and friends were all delighted at the news — all, that is, except my mother. She was a very discerning woman and took a very skeptical view of 'altar calls' and 'sinner's prayers'. At the time, I felt it was sour grapes on her part because I had not been saved in the 'Gospel Hall' or in the exact way that she expected. I did all in my power to prove her wrong! I was soon baptised and accepted into membership at the Baptist Church. Soon I was teaching in Sunday School, telling my testimony and preaching the gospel under the guidance of one of the elders of the Church who took me with him on preaching visits.

When I started work at sixteen in the famous Shorts Aircraft factory, I lost no time witnessing to work-mates about the gospel. A group of us, who were professing Christians, had a Bible Study and a time of prayer each lunchtime. We used to be called 'Holy Joe' and various other derogatory names. It didn't bother me — I was happy to stand up for the Lord Jesus.

Life was to change dramatically in 1959. Firstly, I married a Salvation Army girl. I was only twenty one at the time. Then disaster struck. Along with 3,000 others, I was made redundant after five years at Shorts. It took me three months to secure another job. It meant moving to Lancashire in England to work for another aircraft company, English Electric. Amazingly the lodgings I moved to in January 1960 were about six doors from the local

Gospel Hall. I went along to the Sunday evening meeting one week. I sat at the back. At the end of the meeting no one made an effort to speak to me so I resolved never to go back. In due course the Company found us a flat and we set up home in England. Not until our daughter was born did we make any effort to link up with a Church in England. We tried various denominations but could not find one we liked. We soon gave up our search. Worldly friends and pleasures were increasingly filling our lives and spiritual things were sadly pushed aside. In 1964 we moved to Rugby in Northamptonshire. Thoughts about God were never far away however. I felt increasingly in my heart that I was not really saved and used to worry about things like the return of the Lord and where I would spend eternity.

Holidays

When we went 'home' to Northern Ireland for holidays we always avoided attending meetings if we could. I remember one such trip in 1966. On the day we were due to leave I had two teeth extracted! No sooner had we arrived at my parent's home than we were told there were special gospel meetings in progress at the time in a place called Gransha. Mother offered to baby-sit for our two children if we would go and hear the preacher. I half-heartedly said that we would maybe get around to going one evening when we had nothing else planned.

Unknown to me, before I arrived my Mother had 'primed the preacher'. He visited the home and invited me to the meetings. I answered, *"My wife will go along one evening"*. He had an answer ready; *"I'm not speaking to your wife just now, it is you I am inviting. How about it?"* I found him hard to refuse and promised I would attend one night. That evening my wife and I retired to bed exhausted. During the night I awoke to find my mouth bleeding quite badly. My wife aroused my parents and they called a local nurse out. She was quite concerned when she had trouble finding a pulse. My father left to call a doctor and I was left alone with my mother.

Although, over the years, deep down in my heart I felt that I was still not saved, my mother was the last person I would have admitted it to. But how God works! Here I was now, fearing the worst, sitting up late at night alone with my mother and, with tears streaming down my face, saying to her, *"Mother, I'm not saved."* As it turned out, the doctor felt it unnecessary to come to the house. I went back to bed and all was well by morning.

After this wake up call I did not need any coaxing to attend the gospel meetings. In fact, both my wife and I went every night from then on. From the first night I was awakened to my need of Christ and began to feel convicted about my sin. During the next two weeks I spent many hours trying to find the way of salvation. Some days I would slip a little Bible into my pocket and lose myself in the long grass in one of the fields on my father's farm. I would read John chapter nineteen, the crucifixion chapter, over and over again, trying to find rest for my troubled soul but all to no avail.

Over these days I did not want food, nor could I sleep. When I did sleep from sheer exhaustion, as soon as I woke up the concern for my soul came flooding back again. It was not that I did not know the scriptures. I had been brought up with the gospel and had even preached it myself. What a hypocrite I had been. I wondered if perhaps I would never be saved. We continued attending the meetings each night. On the Thursday before we were due to travel back to England, I spoke to the preacher on the way out of the meeting. *"We are going home tomorrow"* I told him. I will always remember his words; *"Ken, if you leave these meetings unsaved, you might never get saved."* I dropped my head, said goodbye and left.

When we arrived at the farm I told my brother, *"You can cancel the flight. We are not going home tomorrow."* Friday night arrived. Afterwards at the farm my wife announced, *"I got saved during the meeting tonight."* What a shock! I did not even know she was concerned about being saved. It hit me like a thunderbolt. Here I was, having known the gospel well for so long and now my wife is saved and I am still lost. Had I played around with my soul for so many years that God had given me up for good?

Over the weekend I continued searching and reading John chapter nineteen. By the following Wednesday I was desperate. I decided to have a talk with the preacher. I found him. I said, *"Jim, I want to be saved"*. His reply startled me. *"Why have you come to me then? I can't save you. I am only the messenger. God is the one that saves. You go home and get your Bible and get alone with God and He will save you. I'll be praying for you."* I was thrown into near despair by this rebuff. I thought this was unkind and unloving. Actually it was wisdom on the preacher's part. If he had sat and tried to 'lead me to Christ' that afternoon I might have made another false profession.

Despair

I went back to the farm hoping to have the matter settled without delay. Later, when the family went out for a drive, I refused to go with them. As the car pulled away I retired to my bedroom, locked the door and dropped to my knees by the bed. I opened the Bible to John nineteen and read the chapter again. Frankly, all seemed so hopeless. I was really in utter despair. *"What can I do now"*, I thought. I have heard God's voice time and time again over the years. The thought came persistently that I must have missed my opportunity to be saved. I have never known such utter helplessness as I did at that moment. I cried bitterly. My mind turned over the problem again. I was a sinner on my way to hell. How could I be saved? Suddenly I saw it. It was a truth I already knew, but it hit me in a new way, almost as if I had never heard it before. I simply saw the truth that Christ died for me. I had known it since childhood, but at that moment it was like a new revelation to me. My burden of sin lifted. I was saved. I could not say anything for a few moments. The simplicity of it all sank in. My first words were, "*Thank you Lord.*"

The joy of the Lord filled me! I ran out of the house but, of course, there was no one to tell! When the family returned it was such a joy to share the story with them and then to tell the preacher at the meeting that night. What a time of rejoicing. How different to my earlier experience. I did not need to prove anything to my mother. I was resting and rejoicing in my Lord and Saviour. There were no doubts. Christ's finished work on the cross was all I needed.

We finally returned home to England. I nearly lost my job after staying for the extra time in Ulster. I told my boss the reason for my delay. He said "*I hope this will not happen again.*" I replied, "*I guarantee it won't!*" The dear believers at the Gospel Hall in Rugby were a great help to us over the next few years. But my greatest debt, humanly speaking, is to my mother. Her discernment, in seeing through my false profession of salvation, was hugely influential in bringing me to a true saving knowledge of the Lord Jesus. I am so grateful to the Lord that she lived long enough to see all her family saved and one of her daughters doing missionary service overseas. To crown it all, my dear father was saved at the age of 81, three months before he died.

A LOST CHURCH MEMBER

by
Doug Kutilek

I grew up in a church-going Baptist family. Among my earliest memories is being in church at age three, and I cannot remember a time after that that I was not taken to meetings on a regular basis. Not only did I go to Sunday School, but during the summer, I also went to Vacation Bible School year after year, and since my mother was a worker in the VBS, my attendance was always perfect.

At home, Bible stories were read to my siblings and me. In short, I grew up learning and believing the Bible and the stories from the Bible that are the regular subjects of children's Sunday School lessons: Adam and Eve, Cain and Abel, Noah, Abraham, Isaac, Jacob, Moses, Joshua, David, Solomon, Jonah, and the rest of the Old Testament characters, and of course the stories of Jesus: walking on water, healing the sick, lame and blind, feeding 5,000, dying on the cross and rising from the dead, and all the rest. There was never any question in my mind that these stories were entirely true — something I still believe to this day.

As I grew up, I learned that it was expected of each person that sometime he would 'go forward' at the end of the meeting and say that he believed in Jesus and wanted to be baptized. I knew this action was expected of me, but I was very introverted and reluctant to become a spectacle in front of the hundreds of people. However, one day I saw an opportunity to fulfill my obligation without having to embarrass myself unduly. One day in Sunday School, when I was about 8 years old, the lesson was on the importance of accepting Christ personally as Saviour and about going forward at the end of the sermon. I learned that a friend of mine planned to do that very thing — go forward. I thought, "*Now I won't have to do it by myself.*" So, we both went forward, filled out 'decision' cards, and had our hands shaken afterward by all the blue-haired old ladies in the congregation and by many others.

Baptism

The following week, the assistant pastor came to the house and spoke to me (with my mother sitting right next to me) about the facts of the gospel and the importance of believing in Jesus. I gave honest mental assent to what he said, and was scheduled for baptism a few weeks later, which took place as planned. And so I became a 'member in good standing' of the largest Baptist church in the city. But...my mental assent to the facts of the gospel was only that: mental assent. There was no conviction of sin, there was no drawing or illumination by the Holy Spirit, there was no repentance, there was no saving faith in Christ, and there was no salvation! And that is how I remained for nine years.

During those nine years, I continued to attend church on a regular basis. When people asked if I was a Christian, I answered, "*Yes, I've been baptized,*" which certainly is not what makes a person a Christian. During those years, I never had any 'doubts' about my salvation (something I rarely thought about). Satan certainly never put any doubts in my heart about salvation. The last thing he wanted was for me to get seriously concerned about my spiritual state, since that might lead to the discovery that I was indeed very much yet in my sins and without forgiveness.

I heard hundreds of sermons and lessons in those years, and heard the truths of the gospel many times, but these had no impact on my sin-darkened soul. And during those years, I never read the Bible, except for once reading Philemon, one of the shortest books in the New Testament, just so I could brag that I had read one book of the Bible. I did take the Bible with me to church week by week, and read the texts being covered in Sunday school, but for all practical purposes, the Bible was a closed book to me.

College

I graduated from High School after the first semester of my senior year and ten days later was enrolled in College (I was in a big hurry to get a law degree in those days). I soon felt overwhelmed by the College experience — the coursework was vastly more demanding than High School. Both personally and socially, I felt very isolated. The only familiar faces in the sea of 14,000 students were friends of my older sister and brother, all at least a year or two older than me (I being just 17¼ years old). In such circumstances, God brought to my mind words from a sermon. The pastor had said, "*If you have troubles in your life, read the Bible. It will help you out.*" What did I have to lose?

I took a New Testament I had received six or seven years earlier as an award for perfect attendance at VBS, but which I had never read, and began with Matthew's Gospel (in private — I was embarrassed for anyone to see me reading the Bible). I was first of all stunned at how many famous proverbs and literary quotes were biblical (how did I get through 17 years of church attendance without discovering this?). But by the time I got to Matthew chapter 5 (the beginning of the famous 'Sermon on the Mount') my attention became focused on another matter — my own sinfulness and guilt. Jesus declared that not only was violating the letter of the law sin, but the desire in the heart to sin was also sin. I had committed no adultery, but the lust certainly was there in my heart. A deep gloom and burden of conviction descended upon me. I was guilty. I knew it, and God knew it. I had offended God. What could I possibly do to set things right with God? I kept reading.

By the time I got to Matthew chapter 11 a few days later, I recognized that I was hopelessly, helplessly lost in my sins. But here I found cause for hope. In verses 28 and 29, Jesus made what is commonly called the 'great invitation': *"Come unto me all ye who labour and are heavy laden, and I will give you rest. Take my yoke upon you and learn of me, for I am meek and lowly in heart and ye shall find rest unto your souls. For my yoke is easy and my burden is light."* I did not hesitate. *"If He is making that offer to me, I will take Him at His word, I must take Him at His word."* So I came. And true to His word, He took away my sin, my guilt, and my burden, and He gave me salvation, eternal life and peace with God.

Struggles

The following months were rather bumpy spiritually for me. I continued to read the New Testament until after about a full year, I had read it all through. The Holy Spirit convicted me of various things in my life, conduct and vocabulary that needed changing, and without any human encouragement, my progress as an obedient Christian was very uneven, with periods of fighting against the Holy Spirit, followed by periods when God seemed to withdraw His presence from my life. I battled with doubts about my salvation at such times.

I had the additional obstacle of some bad teaching. I had been taught as a child that it was not possible to be certain of one's salvation, and that to say *"I know that I am saved"* was a mark of pride and arrogance. This, combined with the Holy Spirit's heavy hand of conviction left me very miserable for over a year, and greatly in doubt about my spiritual state. Some 15 months after my conversion, a co-worker was saved at his aunt's funeral. He shortly thereafter invited me to a Bible study with the preacher who had pointed him to Christ. I went as a favour to the man, not expecting to get anything out of it. I went and was amazed. Here were about 20 people studying the Bible — and it was interesting, unlike the very dull and poor teaching in the high school and college classes at the church I attended.

I started going regularly to these Friday night Bible studies, then began going to the preacher's Sunday school class. I was now receiving the personal encouragement to live a consistent Christian life that I had needed for over a year. I began to drop various activities and people from my life and began to actively share my faith with people at work, at school, and at city parks. For several weeks, I spent much time in the afternoons in agonizing prayer. After such a struggle, I came to assurance that I did possess salvation, and had for a year and a half. I also soon realized that I had not been baptized after salvation (the universal biblical pattern), and I presented myself for baptism.

So, I found salvation through reading the Gospels for myself. Now I constantly urge others to read them personally, and not to trust what others say about them. When I was eight, I did what others expected of me, and became a 'lost church member'. When at 17 I read the New Testament for myself, I did what the Lord expected of me and became a child of God.

THREE KINDS OF FAITH

by
Michael Penfold

If salvation depended on religious sincerity and knowledge, the Jewish ruler called Nicodemus would certainly have qualified. Yet the Lord Jesus said to this morally upright man, "*You must be born again*". This 'birth' terminology helps us to understand true salvation. A baby is in the dark one minute and in the light the next. Similarly the new birth happens at a moment in time. While there may be a period of conviction and growth in understanding what the gospel is, the actual new birth always takes place in an instant. However, natural birth and spiritual birth can also stand in contrast to one another. Natural birth is something you can never remember; spiritual birth is something you can never forget.

Marriage serves as another good analogy of salvation. At a moment in time a lady answers the question, "*Will you take this man to be your lawful wedded husband*", with the answer, "*I will*". Could Rebecca ever forget the day she decided to marry Isaac, saying "*I will go with this man*"? The five testimonies in this book show how it is quite possible to look, sound and act like a Christian, without actually being one. The Lord Jesus, in His teaching, constantly drew attention to this fact. He spoke of *two trees* that looked very similar. But in the end one was corrupt, as seen by its fruit. Then

He spoke of *two houses* that outwardly appeared the same. No one could tell them apart until the storm came, when one was revealed to have been built on a false foundation. Next, He drew attention to *two crops* growing in the same field. The wheat and the tares looked very similar at the start, but their real identity was discovered and dealt with at the harvest. Christ continues to labour this point with the parable about the *two types of virgins* in Matthew ch. 25, who were very much like each other until midnight when half of them were found out. Later in the same prophetic section of Matthew, the Lord speaks of *two animals* — sheep and goats (which in Israel look quite similar) — and at the judgment of the nations, the sheep enter everlasting bliss but the goats go into everlasting torment.

As a warning to His many false followers, the Lord preached what we seldom hear today — a message about the real agony that accompanies true conversion. He urged his listeners to *"Strive to enter in at the narrow gate"*. To his Middle Eastern hearers this would have come over as *"agonize to enter in"*. This is in stark contrast to the 'just raise your hand', 'come down the front', 'sign a card', 'shake the preacher's hand', 'say this prayer after me' and similar invitations that are now so common. Biblical exposition emphasises awakening, conviction and repentance — elements that are missing in much of today's preaching, thereby producing a crop of false professions.

Salvation is not a reward for anxiety, but conviction of sin is an *essential stage* in the journey of a soul from being dead in sins to being alive in Christ. That said, it does *not* have to continue for a long period of time. On the day of Pentecost 3,000 people were awakened, convicted and saved in the course of one day. The Bible says they were *"pricked in their hearts"* (Acts 2v37). The Greek here means to 'pierce thoroughly or agitate violently'. That was the result of the Holy Spirit's conviction through Peter's preaching.

To understand this whole matter, there is nothing better or more helpful than a thorough grasp of the parable of the sower. There can be no doubt about the interpretation of this parable since the Lord gives us its meaning. The first three ground-types are pictures of the hearts of unregenerate sinners. Only the good ground represents the true believer. The first ground, the 'wayside', depicts a person who is hard-hearted and has no room for the seed of the word. Such a person is clearly not saved. However, the next two types of ground, the 'shallow' and the 'thorny', represent people who at first appear to be genuine converts.

Notice how the rocky shallow ground receives the seed and quickly produces a crop. Here is someone who receives the gospel with excitement and joy (Luke 8v13). However, after the initial burst of encouraging growth, the crop withers because the roots are not deep enough to withstand the heat of the sun. Outwardly everything seemed fine at first, but the Lord says of the shallow stony ground hearers that they *"believe for a while"*. What kind of belief is this? We could call this *emotional faith*, unaccompanied by any depth of reality. Yes, there are often tears when a soul is saved — but mere emotion, such as can be produced by mighty eloquence or musically accompanied appeals, will always result in false short-lived professions. Are we supposed to receive the gospel with excitement? No, it is received with sorrow, brokenness and repentance. When the gospel is gladly received (Acts 2v41, I Thess 1v6) the joy comes from the relief of the burden of sin removed and the assurance of salvation. After being saved, the Chancellor in Acts 8 *"went on his way rejoicing"*.

What was the problem with the shallow ground? It had never been ploughed up. Before the seed can drop into the hardened heart of the sinner his heart must be ploughed up by exposure to God's law. By the law is the knowledge of sin (Romans 3v20). What a wonderful preparatory job such an exposition of man's lost condition does. How it prepares the ground for the good news of redeeming grace.

However, at many evangelistic crusades, people sit through the entertainment set before them, hear a brief gospel message and, with no deep ploughing of conviction by the Holy Spirit through an exposition of sin, righteousness and judgment to come, they receive the word with joy. It springs up. It looks promising. But, as anyone knows who has looked at the fine print, anywhere from 80-100% of those who 'go forward' are often never seen again. Their response is purely emotional The September 1977 issue of *Eternity Magazine* reported the results of an evangelistic crusade that involved 178 churches. Out of 4,106 decisions, only 3% joined a local church. That series of meetings created 3,983 'backsliders'. These figures are typical of modern mass evangelism.

The third type, the 'thorny' ground, produces no more fruit than the first two. The crop is choked. This depicts those who hear the word and may well give mental assent to the gospel but life continues as busy as ever and no fruit is forthcoming. They may even have an outward conformity to Christianity — but no inward reality. Such people have what we could call *intellectual faith*. They are able to argue the case for the existence of God, the reliability of the Bible and they believe in creation rather than evolution. But their mental assent to 'the truth' is not true salvation. Their real concern in life is business, money and pleasure (Luke 8v14). They have never been converted and if they honestly examined their priorities and ambitions, their true standing before God would become blindingly obvious to them.

Reader, where do *you* stand today? Was your conversion mere emotion, or have you perhaps just an intellectual conformist type of faith? Have you just mentally assented to factual information, without the truth ever really gripping your heart and changing your life? No deep work of the Spirit, no sense of guilt, no brokenness, no moment of time when you were truly converted. Will you be with those who say *"Lord, Lord"* yet in reply He will say, *"Depart from Me, I never knew you"*? Are you just the same person you always were, or have you ever truly become a new creature in Christ (II Corinthians 5v17)?

The third and only *true* kind of faith is found in Acts 20v21, where salvation is described as *"Repentance toward God and faith toward our Lord Jesus Christ."* This is **saving faith**. A conscious change of mind about sin and unbelief together with the exercise of complete faith in Christ alone. It is pictured in the good ground, the fourth type of soil in the parable of the sower. Yet this is where so many go astray. Exactly what does it mean to believe? The following is a true story. A young man was approached by a worried elderly lady. This lady had come in contact with a Christian who had asked her when she was saved. The elderly lady had been confused and unable to reply (she was a very religious woman — but had never been born again). The young man, in an attempt to console this troubled lady, asked her a question; *"Do you believe Christ died for you?"* The anxious lady replied, *"Yes"*. *"Well,"* said the young man, *"You are saved then."* What was wrong with his answer? It showed a lack of understanding of the nature of believing. Millions of people who 'believe' Christ died for them are not saved. Why? Because they believe Christ died for them in the same way that they believe the soldiers who went to the beaches in Normandy on D-Day in 1944 died for them. They believe it as a historical fact — nothing more. It makes no difference to their daily behaviour or lifestyle.

Let me illustrate it using a seafaring analogy. Suppose you are standing safely on the deck of a ship. I say to you, pointing at the life-belt, *"Do you believe that life-belt can save you?"* *"Yes,"* you say, *"I do."* Are you saved by this acknowledgment? Of course not.

Now, try to imagine having been washed overboard on a stormy night. You are in danger of imminent death by drowning. A lifeboat pulls alongside and a life-belt is thrown towards you. Without a moment's thought about 'believing' or 'not believing', you immediately rest all your hopes on the life belt by grabbing it and hugging it to yourself. At that precise moment, you have moved from a mere intellectual belief in life-belts to a personal experience of being saved by a life-belt. You believed to the point that you acted on that conviction and took hold of it for yourself.

It is the same with salvation. There is more than 'just believing'. When a person is awakened, convicted and comes to a proper realization of their lost condition, then they are in a position to be truly saved. For as long as I can remember, I believed Christ died for me. I never had a problem with that. But I was not saved until from a broken and contrite spirit I ceased my weary trying and struggling and rested all on Christ for salvation. May you, dear reader, rest there too for eternity.

The Test Most Christians Never Take

Since 1st John was written *"That ye may know that ye have eternal life"* (I John 5v13), why don't you take the 12 point test outlined in John's epistle? Do you have:

1. A saving faith in Christ - I John 5v13?
2. A personal relationship with the Father & Son - I John 1v2-3?
3. A sensitivity to sin - I John 1v5-10?
4. A desire to be obedient to God - I John 2v3-6?
5. A love of the Father rather than the world - I John 2v15-17?
6. An expectant anticipation of Christ's return - I John 3v2-3?
7. A decreasing pattern of sin in your life - I John 3v4-9?
8. A experience of the fact that the world hates you - I John 3v13?
9. A love for the believers - I John 3v14?
10. Regular answered prayer - I John 3v22, 5v14-15?
11. Discernment of error and false doctrine - I John 4v1-3, 6?
12. The witness of the Holy Spirit within you - I John 5v10?

If you can honestly pass these tests you can indeed know that you have eternal life.

If you have just trusted Christ as your Lord and Saviour:

After coming to know Christ as your Lord and Saviour, you should immediately take the following steps:

1) Thank Him for what He has done for you and ask yourself the question, "*What can I now do for Him.*"

2) Start speaking daily to Him in prayer from your heart, bringing Him praise and thanksgiving, as well as asking Him for blessings.

3) Get a Bible and start reading and studying it. It's best to begin with the Gospels (e.g. Mark or John) and read through the New Testament. Ask God to give you understanding on how to apply it practically to your life.

4) Find a Bible believing church and attend its meetings every week.

4) Tell others what the Lord has done for you.

If you would like confidential help or further information, please feel free to contact us. We can supply you with a free Bible, a correspondence course and an address of a Bible believing church in your area. Our address is:

Penfold Books
P.O.Box 26, Bicester, Oxon, OX26 4GL, England.
Tel: + 44 (0) 1869 249574 Fax: + 44 (0) 1869 244033
E-mail: penfoldbooks@characterlink.net
Web: www.penfoldbooks.com

If this book has been a help to you please let us know
We greatly value the feedback we receive from our readers

Acknowledgements:

Permission to publish the testimonies in this book was granted to us freely by each individual author. We acknowledge our gratefulness to them for kindly agreeing to help in this project.

Also available:

Dawn of the New Age
5 New Agers relate their search for the truth

Angels of Light
5 Spiritualists test the Spirits

Messiah
5 Jewish people make the greatest discovery

Available from bookshops or direct from the publishers.

Published by:
Penfold Books
P.O. Box 26, Bicester, Oxon, OX26 4GL, England
Tel: + 44 (0) 1869 249574   Fax: + 44 (0) 1869 244033
Email: penfoldbooks@characterlink.net
Web: www.penfoldbooks.com

ISBN: 1-900742-11-X